LEARNING FROM
"LEARNING BY DOING"
Lessons for Economic Growth

The Kenneth J. Arrow Lectures

LEARNING FROM
"LEARNING BY DOING"

Lessons for Economic Growth

ROBERT M. SOLOW

《 》

Stanford University Press
Stanford, California

Stanford University Press
Stanford, California
© 1997 by the Board of Trustees of the
Leland Stanford Junior University
Printed in the United States of America

CIP data appear at the end of the book

Stanford University Press publications are
distributed exclusively by Stanford
University Press within the United States,
Canada, Mexico, and Central America;
they are distributed exclusively by
Cambridge University Press throughout
the rest of the world.

PREFACE

The first two chapters of this little book are the Arrow Lectures I delivered in 1993 at the invitation of the Stanford Economics Department. I am grateful to Professor Gavin Wright and my other Stanford colleagues for giving me the opportunity to pay tribute to a splendid economist and a friend of 40-plus years, and for the delightful few days my wife and I spent in Palo Alto on that occasion. The lectures are printed more or less exactly as I delivered them. This is not the result of mere laziness. I like the informal tone of spoken lectures because I fear that the formal style of journal articles and treatises tends to disguise the essentially exploratory, almost playful, character of all theory and makes it look more self-important than it can possibly be.

It was clear to me from the start that the story I was telling would benefit from some numerical explorations. So, when Stanford University Press expressed an interest in publishing the lectures, I decided to complete them with a third "virtual" lecture describing the results of a series of computer simulations. The programming and computing were carried out by Eileen Brooks, then a senior at MIT. She did the job with abundant intelligence, understanding, and energy. I want to thank Lee Ward for preparing the figures in Chapter 3 and Ellen F. Smith of Stanford University Press for an excellent and (at least for me) painless job of editing.

The Press suggested that the book would be better if it contained some remarks about economic policy. I experience a mild allergic reaction from contact with solemn policy implications drawn from untested, or superficially tested, or non-robust theoretical exercises. (Needless to say, I itch a lot.) So I decided instead to include an earlier paper containing some general reflections on policies for economic growth, drawn not from any one modeling exercise but from general experience with a variety of growth models. The Johns Hopkins School of Advanced International Studies in Washington was generous enough to allow me to reprint the Ernest Sturc Lecture given there in 1991 and issued as a separate pamphlet by the School at that time. I hope it strikes the right note.

As usual, and more so with every passing year, I owe a debt of gratitude to Aase Huggins and Janice Murray for typing the manuscript, getting it in shape, and generally making sure that I do not zig when I should be zagging. Everyone should be so lucky.

R.M.S.

« »

CONTENTS

LEARNING FROM "LEARNING BY DOING"

Lessons for Economic Growth

1 «»

LEARNING BY DOING
IN THE CONTEXT OF
GROWTH THEORY

In olden days, professors of economics did research and wrote papers on their own time. Topics suggested themselves in the way I imagine that themes came to Schubert: not exactly out of the blue, because everyone has a history and everything has a context, but out of some variable mixture of one's internal and external environment. In those days, invitations to give lectures or write something for a conference were rare. We produced to stock, not to order. I liked that system. Intellectual production to order can lead to scraping the bottom of the barrel. Not always, of course: you can think of the Goldberg Variations as an astonishing counterexample, along with the Diabelli Variations. But the fact that both pieces of music are sets of variations is suggestive.

When I was invited to give these Arrow Lectures, I felt led, as if by a visible hand, to a preordained topic. Amartya Sen must have felt he was merely falling in with the established order of things and that he had no choice but to talk about social choice. Frank Hahn would have felt that he had disturbed a carefully arranged equilibrium if he had talked about anything else but general equilibrium theory. And somehow the phrase "learning by doing" appeared in my mind before I even began to think. It was clear from the start that this was meant to be an opportunity for me to do some learning by lecturing.

The opportunity is more than welcome. "The Economic Implications of Learning by Doing" (1962) is almost certainly Arrow's most important piece of middlebrow theory. It is true that there is not a lot of middlebrow theory in the Arrow canon. But the 1962 paper is an important one by any standard. It is always cited as an ancestor in the founding works of the "new" or "endogenous" growth theory. It is, in fact, a little more than just an ancestor. One of the points I intend to make in this lecture is that Arrow's paper comes very close to anticipating New Growth Theory. It is tempting to conclude that Arrow could have anticipated New Growth Theory if he had felt like it, so to speak; and that some implicit instinct might have kept him from doing so. It is a question worth thinking about whether that instinct was a good one or not, whether the version of growth theory that Arrow shied away from, the road not taken, leads in the right direction.

My plan in this chapter is to begin with an exposition of "The Economic Implications of Learning by Doing," because not everyone will be familiar with it. This exposition will be brief and selective. Anyone can read the whole paper; I want to stand on its shoulders. Then I shall focus on the relation of Arrow's model to at least one branch of the New Growth Theory, showing how it is a sort of prototype and how it turns away from being more than a prototype. Of course, we cannot know whether it was a turning away or a not noticing. I first read the paper 30 years ago, and I do not remember noticing that it contained a remarkable special case. Actually, there is internal evidence that Arrow did not notice either; that is why I spoke of an "implicit" instinct. After that, I will try to use Arrow's paper as a springboard for a critical consideration of the spectacular recent developments that have made growth theory a hot topic again. And, finally, I will suggest a rather different direction in which the learning-by-doing model might be developed, which is, in fact, the subject of the second chapter.

Arrow's 1962 paper is explicitly motivated by the wish to convert the level of technology into an endogenous element in the theory of economic growth. It was hardly a novel idea that technological progress cannot be wholly exogenous. Business firms (and sometimes individuals) spend valuable resources in the hope of acquiring even more valuable technological knowledge. They are seeking a pecuniary return, and sometimes they succeed. That observation by itself butters no parsnips. It leads somewhere only if it is accompanied by a useful thought about how to model the process of acquiring new technology.

One way to proceed is to treat industrial research as a costly but profit-seeking activity. Interestingly enough, Arrow does not do that. Instead he moves at once to the idea of learning rather than invention. And he emphasizes the common belief among psychologists that "learning is the product of experience." (Characteristically, he refers to literature outside of economics, in particular to Ernest Hilgard's textbook on learning theory and Wolfgang Köhler's Gestalt ideas; not to John Dewey, however.)

What really matters is that he has in mind a way to represent the dependence of the level of technology on the experience of production. That, too, he relates to something outside of conventional economics: the fact—well known around the RAND Corporation at the time—that the direct labor requirement to build an airframe seems quite regularly to fall as a function of *cumulative* output, with an elasticity of about (minus) one-third. This regularity was called a "learning curve" by practitioners. So the idea is to build a model embodying the hypothesis that the experience of production carries with it, as a by-product, an automatic improvement in productivity, what we might as well think of as technological progress. Of course, once this is known, market decisions will take it into account as one of the benefits of production, just as airframe manufacturers used the learning-curve concept in projecting costs and making bids.

Arrow chose to treat gross investment as the vehicle through which learning occurs. Capital equipment comes in units of equal (infinitesimal) size, and the productivity achievable using any unit of equipment depends on how much investment had already occurred when this particular unit was produced. The key point is that productivity advances rapidly during intervals of high investment and slowly (or not at all) when gross investment is slow (or absent). Even without a deliberate "research" activity, the time rate of change of productivity is endogenous in the proper sense that it depends on economic decisions, in this case the decision to buy new capital equipment.

The airframe learning curve had been couched in terms of cumulative output, not cumulative investment; and the intuitive notion of "experience" is more naturally caught by cumulative output than by cumulative investment. After all, the operator of a particular machine becomes more proficient with experience. Arrow offers a brief explanation of his switch, which excludes this sort of learning, but it now seems cryptic to me. I prefer to give credit to the middlebrow theorist's instinct. When you work it out, the use of investment leads to a more interesting model. Perhaps it also matters that cumulative investment has a sort of narrative reality. After correction for depreciation, it represents a mixed stock of capital goods, whereas cumulative output is just an integral. Correspondingly, the choice of cumulative investment makes a tacit appeal to the intuitive "vintage" notion, that up-to-date technology is embodied in currently produced equipment. All in all, it tells a better story.

The 1962 model makes use of a vintage model with fixed coefficients (used also in Solow, Tobin, von Weizsäcker, and Yaari, 1965), offering only a bow to the possibility of ex post substitution between labor and capital of a given vintage. (David Levhari looked at generalizations in this direction a few years later.) Thus, given any history of gross investment up to the present moment, with a newer vintage always more profitable to use than any earlier vintage, one can calculate directly how much labor is needed to operate all of the equipment starting at the newest and going back to older and older vintages. The boundary separating usable from obsolete equipment is reached when this process has employed all the available labor. (The competitive equilibrium product-wage falls out of this calculation in the obvious Ricardian way; it leaves zero rent at the margin of obsolescence.) Then it is possible to add up the output produced by operation of all the economically viable equipment. Any story that divides aggregate output between immediate consumption and gross investment will push the investment profile forward to the next instant of time. The supply of labor may grow also, according to its own rules. The stage is then set to repeat the process I have just described. At least for this full-employment case we have the makings of a determinate growth model.

The very last paragraph of Arrow's paper reads as follows: "It has been assumed here that learning takes place only as a by-product of ordinary production. In fact, society has created institutions, education and research, whose purpose is to enable learning to take place more rapidly. A fuller model would take account of these as additional variables." Indeed the growth theory literature has done just that, but not yet in a clearly convincing way, at least not to me. I do not want to encroach seriously on that territory now, any more than Arrow did 30 years ago, though I will return to this point from a different angle later on.

Arrow does most of his analysis with a highly concrete specification of the model, and I shall follow him, though it is possible to get pretty far with a more general version. Here I have to reproduce a few equations.

Let $g(t)$ be the rate of gross investment at time t and let $G(t)$ be the cumulative gross investment from the "beginning" up to time t. It does not matter when the beginning actually was, because under full-employment growth only a fraction of the equipment ever built is operational, the rest being obsolete in the sense that all of the available labor is used up in operating more recent and therefore more productive and more profitable equipment. Arrow's specification of the learning process goes like this. Every unit of investment of any vintage yields exactly a units of output per unit time as long as it is operational, and then of course zero when it is obsolete. A unit of investment created when the cumulative total of past investment was G requires bG^{-n} units of labor to operate it. So learning is labor saving but output neutral. The intensity of labor saving corresponds to the commonly used airframe function (where, as I mentioned, n is typically about 1/3). It is possible to work out the case where learning is output increasing instead of (or as well as) labor saving, but I shall not pursue this extra generality. So the margin of obsolescence G' is determined by setting

$$(1) \qquad L = b \int_{G'}^{G} g^{-n} dg .$$

Equipment built when cumulative investment was less than G' is obsolete. And then the current rate of output is given by

$$(2) \qquad x = a(G - G').$$

Solving (1) for G' and substituting in (2) leads to a sort-of-but-not-quite production function

$$(3) \qquad x = aG \left[1 - \left(1 - \frac{L}{cG^{1-n}} \right)^{1/(1-n)} \right]$$

so long as $n \neq 1$, where $c = b/(1 - n)$. I will come to the case $n = 1$ in due course. This is not quite a production function, because G is not quite a factor of production. There is no point in asking for a "stock of capital," because capital equipment is not homogeneous, and in any case G will do quite well when it comes to answering questions about wages and profits.

Now Arrow remarks that this "production function" exhibits increasing returns to scale in G and L whether $n < 1$ or $n > 1$. He is right, of course, but I am going to argue that the case $n > 1$ is very peculiar, and the model makes sense only with $n \leq 1$. This amendment is more than merely technical. It alerts us to the notion that $n = 1$ is an extreme case, not something intermediate and therefore hardly special.

The simplest hint that there is something disreputable about $n > 1$ comes from the airframe learning curve itself. The original empirical finding was that the direct labor input required to produce the kth in a sequence of identical airframes was proportional to k^{-n} with $n \cong 1/3$. Equivalently, the total labor input required to produce the first k airframes is proportional to $1/1 + 1/2^n + 1/3^n + \ldots + 1/k^n$. Now suppose that $n > 1$. Students of calculus, at least old students of calculus, will remember that the infinite series $\sum_{k=1}^{\infty} k^{-n}$ converges if $n > 1$ and diverges if $n \leq 1$. The implication is that if $n > 1$, it takes only a finite amount of labor to produce an infinite number of airframes. To put it more precisely, $n > 1$ implies that there is a certain number of labor hours $\overline{L}$ with the property that no sequence of airframes, no matter how long, will ever require as many as $\overline{L}$ hours of labor to complete. That seems to contradict the whole idea of scarcity. The empirical value $n = 1/3$ is safely away from the extreme.

The not-quite-production-function (3) makes purely algebraic sense whether n is greater than or smaller than one. (The borderline case $n = 1$ is still reserved for later discussion.) If $0 < n < 1$, L is less than cG^{1-n} because the latter is the employment that would be required to operate *all* past gross investment and L is by definition just enough to operate the nonobsolescent portion. If $n > 1$, $c = b/(1-n)$ is negative and the whole expression in the inner parenthesis exceeds unity; it is raised to a negative power and so output is again safely positive.

Direct calculation gives us the "marginal product" of G. It is

(4)
$$\frac{\partial x}{\partial G} = 1 - \left(1 - \frac{L}{cG^{1-n}}\right)^{\frac{n}{1-n}}.$$

This too is positive for n on either side of one. (The same is true of the marginal product of labor: the availability of a little more labor will shift the margin of obsolescence backward and increase output.)

Another differentiation gives us

(5) $$\frac{\partial^2 x}{\partial G^2} = -\frac{nL}{c} G^{n-2} \left(1 - \frac{L}{cG^{1-n}}\right)^{\frac{2n-1}{1-n}}.$$

Now there is something to notice. If $n < 1$, the expression is negative; there are diminishing returns to gross investment and nothing to write home about. If $n > 1$, however, the sign changes. There are increasing returns to G. There are indeed increasing returns to scale in both cases, but that does not matter very much. What does matter is the presence of increasing returns to G alone. How does it matter?

There is a qualitative hint in the earlier remark about the learning curve: that $n > 1$ allows infinite output with a finite amount of labor (and no other factor of production). A further hint appears in Arrow's own calculations. He asks whether exponential steady-state growth is possible in this model if L grows exponentially at any given rate. Suppose that a fixed fraction of output becomes gross investment. Then, if output is to grow exponentially, investment must grow exponentially and at the same rate. A glance at the not-quite-production-function tells us that L and G^{1-n} must grow at the same rate. Now everything clicks into place. If employment and labor force grow at the rate γ, output and investment must grow at the rate $\gamma/(1 - n)$.

Bells should go off. If $n < 1$ everything is fine. There is a unique steady-state configuration. Its growth rate has just been determined, depending only on employment growth and the learning parameter. The levels of output and investment are determined by the investment quota, say s. This is the standard pattern familiar from Old Growth Theory, as Arrow explained in 1962.

Here I can go a step further than Arrow did. He remarks that he has not investigated the stability of the steady state whose existence he has ascertained, even in the base case of a constant rate of gross investment. Stability is not automatic, because of increasing return to scale, even when $n < 1$. It happens, however, that the Arrow model falls into a class that can be directly analyzed. The key observation is that the right-hand side of (3) is homogeneous of degree one in the variables G and $L^{1/1-n}$. This fact allows a fairly standard argument to show that paths with a constant rate of gross investment all converge to an appropriate steady state, provided $n < 1$. The resemblance to Old Growth Theory is complete, except for the important shift from autonomous technological progress to learning by investing.

But if $n > 1$, the same argument tells us that the only exponential steady state is one in which exponentially growing employment is accompanied by exponentially falling investment and output. Arrow never notices this explicitly. My presumption is that he avoided this case intuitively, the way an experienced helmsman will avoid a patch of submerged rocks in a familiar harbor.

But of course, once you focus on this perverse case, you see that it is warning that something is wrong, just the way youthful hydraulic Keynesians used to learn not to take literally the "negative multiplier" associated with a marginal propensity to spend bigger than one. In Arrow's case the interpretation is that there is no meaningful exponential steady state. In fact an economy with learning elasticity $n > 1$ would explode to infinite output in finite time, and that is well beyond exponential. The case $n > 1$ is, to put it mildly, impractical. It seems, as I noted earlier, inconsistent with the idea of scarcity and therefore with the idea of economics.

If I have succeeded in characterizing learning elasticities smaller than one as easy to live with and learning elasticities larger than one as impossible to live with, then the case $n = 1$

is the borderline. It is either the least impossible impossible case or the least easy easy case. The time has obviously come to look at this case explicitly.

Obviously one cannot just set $n = 1$ in the not-quite-production-function (3), keeping in mind that $c = b/(1 - n)$. But it is simple either to start over with (1) and (2) or to do a limiting process in (3). The result, which appears in the 1962 article, is

$$(6) \qquad x = aG(1 - e^{-L/b}).$$

It takes no calculation to see that this has a positive and diminishing marginal product of labor. The interesting thing is that it is linear in G. As usual the important characteristic of the model is not that it continues to exhibit increasing returns to scale (as it does) but that this borderline case has exactly constant returns to cumulated gross investment. The case of a unit learning elasticity thus leads directly to one of the simpler forms of the New Growth Theory.

The main implication of linearity is perfectly obvious. Suppose that a given fraction s of current output is turned into gross investment. Then it follows from (6) that the rate of growth of G is $sa(1 - e^{-L/b})$. So the rate of growth of G depends on the investment quota s in every run. Actually one can say a lot more. There is no literal exponential steady state in this model unless employment is constant; but if the volume of employment increases over time, exponentially or not, the model economy gets closer and closer to a steady state. The rate of growth of cumulated investment increases through time. The rate of growth of output is always a little larger than that for cumulative investment. But both of them converge to a constant steady-state rate of growth and that rate is sa, which is exactly what my old friend and colleague Evsey

Domar would have said almost 50 years ago. The steady-state growth rate in this special case is the product of an investment quota and an incremental output-capital ratio. What goes around comes around.

Learning by doing with $n = 1$ thus turns out to be a prototypical New Growth Theory model (one of a class usually called "AK models" because of their linearity with respect to capital). Among New Growth Theorists it is common practice to replace the arbitrary investment quota by a story in which the economy carries out the infinite-time, perfect-foresight, intertemporal optimization program of an immortal individual or dynasty. I find that I resist this practice instinctively. It seems to me foolish to interpret as a descriptive theory what my generation learned from Frank Ramsey to treat as a normative theory, a story about what an omniscient, omnipotent, and nevertheless virtuous planner would do. That is what Arrow does in the 1962 paper; I do not know if he still clings to the old ways, like me. It is not a matter of great importance for growth theory. The two approaches come to the same thing in the long run, although they can differ in the short run.

You see now what I meant when I said at the beginning that Arrow could have anticipated the New Growth Theory if he had felt like it. Equation (6) appears in his paper, and later on he sometimes, but not always, makes a point of recording what happens in the special case $n = 1$. He never considers separately the cases where n exceeds 1. The section of the paper in which Arrow lays out the relations characterizing steady-state growth are silent about alternative values of n. He must have been thinking exclusively in terms of the well-behaved case $n < 1$, else he would surely have been drawn up short by the appearance of negative growth rates.

Here is another piece of textual evidence. When he has completed his survey of steady-state properties of the full-employment version of the model (the only one I am considering here), Arrow remarks: "As in many growth models, the rates of growth of the variables in this system do not depend on savings behavior; however, their levels do." That is, of course, a true statement if $n < 1$, but not otherwise.

I have attributed Arrow's failure to pick up on the special properties associated with $n = 1$ (not to mention $n > 1$) to a theorist's instinct. The question now has to be faced: was his instinct right in passing up the chance to anticipate this version of New Growth Theory? Or would it be more accurate to replace the phrase "theorist's instinct" by Veblen's sardonic notion of a "trained incapacity." I do not want to proceed to a full-dress consideration of this complicated question, but there are some judgments that emerge naturally from reading and thinking about the learning-by-doing paper, and those seem to belong in this context, although their implications extend generally into growth theory.

The first point I want to make seems to me to be very important; but the fact that it is apparently never discussed makes me wonder if I may be wrong about its significance. It is that the key hypothesis underlying at least the "AK" version of New Growth Theory is completely nonrobust. Nature must do exactly the right thing or else the theory evaporates in one way or another. A theory so precariously balanced owes us a powerful reason why Nature should be so obliging.

The groundwork for this remark has already been laid, but I will be explicit about it, even at the cost of some repetition. If the elasticity of the learning curve is less than 1, the Arrow model is a contribution to Old Growth Theory. It adds something new and different to that theory. But it passes the litmus test for belonging: a spontaneous or policy-induced change in the rate of investment does not change the rate of growth, but only the level of the whole steady-state path. Alternatively, if the elasticity of the learning curve exceeds one, the Arrow model—and not only the Arrow model—produces a sort of Big Bang that robs it of plausibility or even of the capacity to represent a world of scarcity. Only if the elasticity of the learning curve is exactly 1 does the model have the New Growth Theory property that a change in the tax rate on the income from capital, or anything else that increases the saving-investment rate, will permanently raise the steady-state growth rate.

I am dramatizing a little. Of course it is true to say that if the learning elasticity is only a tiny bit bigger than 1, it will take a long time for the Big Bang to become visible; output will grow to infinity in finite time, but a long finite time. But that still does not allow a lot of leeway; n will have to be almost equal to 1. The model is perhaps not completely nonrobust; it is just not robust.

What I have said about the Arrow model is true more generally. There is a large subclass of the New Growth Theory that plays on the assumed proportionality of output and capital, a Domar-like route to a Domar-like result. Go one step further, however, and let the elasticity of output with respect to capital exceed unity, and the Big Bang appears on the road ahead; a constant rate of investment is enough to produce an infinite amount of output in finite time.

The world could just happen to be exactly like that. But you would have to be a real plunger to rest the theory of economic growth on one powerful long-shot coincidence. Newton's inverse square law of gravitational attraction sounds like just such a long shot. A physicist friend tells me, however, that Newton's universe would not collapse if the correct statement happened to involve the inverse 2.1 or 1.9 power. It might be less beautiful, no doubt. Those neatly closed elliptical orbits would precess quite a lot. In fact, the relativistic corrections that led to Einstein's famous prediction of the precession of the orbit of Mercury function rather like minor deviations from the inverse square law. No doubt larger deviations could lead to a radically stranger universe or to an unstable one. Nevertheless Newton seems to have allowed the universe considerably more leeway than the New Growth Theory does, and this despite the fact that I am somehow more prepared to accept the exact inverse square law of gravitational attraction as a fact of nature than I am the exact proportionality of output with respect to accumulatable factors of production.

Is the assumption of constant returns *to scale* the same sort of nonrobust assumption, only in this case the one that pervades Old Growth Theory? Constant returns to scale is certainly a borderline case, unlikely to turn up in practice. The difference is that Old Growth Theory can live comfortably with increasing or decreasing returns to scale. It is true that if we insist on generating exponential steady states, non–constant returns to scale have to enter in a certain special way; but that is purely a matter of convenience and does not affect fundamentals.

All in all, I am left with the feeling that the "AK" version of New Growth Theory depends on the universal occurrence of an unexplained fluke. So far, then, Arrow's instinct was sound. It is necessary to go further, however, and ask if there is any strong empirical backing for the presumption of constant returns to the collection of reproducible factors of production. My tentative impression is that there is not. To tell the

)uld be all but impossible to make a convincing
;e. Observations consistent with constant returns
_µital would inevitably also be consistent with a fair range
of increasing and decreasing returns to capital. But both of
those alternatives spell trouble for the theory. That is precisely
what makes nonrobust theories such a pain in the neck in an
inexact science. They require more faith than is healthy for an
economist.

Actually, the empirical situation is even less favorable than
that. The standard empirical exercise is a cross-country regression that has the rate of growth of real output (averaged
over some interval of time) as the dependent variable. The
explanatory variables include the sorts of things that would
indeed help to determine the permanent rate of growth in the
special case of constant returns to reproducible capital but
would be responsible only for transitory effects under diminishing returns. The uncovering of a strong, stable relationship
could perhaps be taken as evidence in favor of the "AK"
model, although the test is pretty indirect. But in point of
fact, such cross-country regressions turn out to be anything
but strong and stable. It would be more accurate to say that
the size and significance of regression coefficients are quite
sensitive to the details of specification: the particular set of independent variables chosen, the sample period, the functional
form of the proposed relation, and variations in econometric
method. Such results are certainly not incompatible with New
Growth Theory, but they are just as certainly not capable of
transforming prior skepticism into posterior conviction.

More recent and slightly more direct tests of the New
Growth Theory seem to come out even worse. The work
of Nazrul Islam, a doctoral student of Dale Jorgenson's at
Harvard, makes use of a combined time-series-cross-section

method and hands down a verdict in favor of Old Growth Theory. This is both good news and bad news. There is not much that policy can do to increase the permanent rate of growth. But then there is not much policy can do to mess things up.

There is, however, a quite different version of New Growth Theory that seems to hold more promise. It tries to do what Arrow did not attempt: that is, to model the process of creating new technology as a special resource-using, profit-seeking activity with its own technology. This branch of the theory endogenizes technological progress, not as a by-product of investment or the routine production of goods, but on its own.

It goes without saying that any such model can be only as convincing as its account of the research and development process. There is no doubt that this line of thought has produced some interesting and even exciting ideas. It is less clear that it has been able to isolate the essential features of the discovery and diffusion of innovations. My impression is that at least some economists who study the historical reality of research and development think that the growth theorists are far enough off the mark to call into question the conclusions they come to.

That may be in part the natural reaction of the close student of institutions and behavior to the necessary abstraction of the theorist. No doubt the theoretical ecologists who write down models of the adaptive reactions of the alligator evoke nothing but contempt from those who study and love the individual beast in its habitat. That is only to be expected. It is never easy to get the two styles to work together, so that the close observer is prepared to say which is the best among the abstractions that will meet the needs of the model builder, while the model builder is prepared to give up a neat and symmetrical formulation for something uglier in the interest of some extra descriptive truth. I do not remember who it was that said that anyone who wants to make the lion lie down with the lamb will need a steady supply of lambs. In this case it is not clear which party is the lion, or the alligator.

Some of the earliest New Growth Theory essays in the modeling of the research process made the same unwise commitment to the singular case of constant returns to accumulatable factors. One sometimes finds, for example, the bald assumption that the *growth rate* of something identified as the stock of "human capital" or "technological knowledge" is a function of the amount of available labor-time spent in training or research. This translates into the differential equation $dH/dt = kHf(L_H)$. The problem here is the same one I identified earlier. Generalize this to the more flexible formulation $dH/dt = kH^m f(L_H)$. Then, if $m < 1$, you will not be surprised to learn, the full model becomes Old Growth Theory in character; it cannot generate sustained productivity growth without an exogenous source of technological progress. If $m > 1$, on the other hand, the model again provides too much bang. Any *constant* allocation of labor L_H to human capital accumulation (or R&D) will drive the stock of human capital (or technological knowledge) to infinity in finite time; under normal assumptions, output goes with it. It is only when $m = 1$ that the model works. Then, of course, it is transparent that the rate of growth of H is just $kf(L_H)$. So a once-for-all change in L_H, which is probably not hard to induce, creates a permanent change in the growth rate of H and thence in the growth rate of aggregate output.

If that were all, the same sort of doubt that applies to "AK" theory would apply here as well: the whole theory would rest on one gratuitous assumption. But fortunately that is not all. The endogenous-innovation branch of the New Growth Theory has been able to go beyond this excessively simple formulation to more complex and interesting stories. The pioneer in this branch, as with the AK version, was Paul Romer; but a great variety of models has been proposed, perhaps too casually. This is what happens when theorists know little about the institutional facts and when those who do know are unwilling or unable to reduce them to the sort of skeleton that a theorist can use. I am not going to pursue this line of thought in any detail, because my main interest is the modeling of economic growth, not the modeling of research and development and the source of technological progress. It is only right, however, that I should acknowledge that I have profited a lot from the work of Gene Grossman and Elhanan Helpman, Philippe Aghion and Peter Howitt, and my former MIT colleague Alwyn Young.

Instead of summarizing at this point, I would rather look ahead and give some indication of the direction in which my argument is going. Arrow's achievement was to construct a growth model—an Old Growth Model—in which technological change was endogenous: internalized but not purposeful. It is a fair comment on this model, as on my own, that the notion of "innovation" has disappeared. That is not necessarily deplorable. It could be, indeed it may be, that the idea of discrete innovation is a valid description of an important process at the microlevel. Even so, when events are aggregated to the scale of the economy as a whole, there may be no real loss in describing the overall "level of technology" as a smooth or mildly irregular function of time or of cumulated gross investment. I can think of two reasons for not leaving it at that, apart from sheer scientific curiosity.

The first has to do with policy. A society that would like to accelerate (or decelerate) the pace of technological progress will need some understanding of the microlevel process in order to design effective incentives or even to make centralized decisions. That is enough reason to get on with the study of research and development, empirically and theoretically. There is, as I have said, an exciting literature along those lines.

The second reason is the one that moves me. It is a thought that has emerged from the many recent studies of the fate of manufacturing industry in the United States, including the inevitable comparisons with Japan. There appear to be two processes at work, not just one. The more obvious one is the occurrence of discrete innovations, some major, some minor, whose development changes the nature of the product or the nature of the production process in existing industries, or may even lead to the creation of recognizably new industries. These innovations are the product, perhaps unintended or unexpected, of an activity that one would clearly describe as research. The less obvious process is usually described as "continuous improvement" of products and processes. It consists of an ongoing series of minor improvements in the design and manufacture of standard products. It leads to advances in customer satisfaction, in quality, durability, and reliability, and to continuing reductions in the cost of production. These improvements usually arise somewhere on or close to the factory floor. They may have absolutely nothing to do with the sort of people who are engaged in research, and they are not the product of a research activity. If one had to give a shorthand description of the process of continuous improvement, "learning by doing" would serve pretty well.

In the next chapter I will try to stretch the Arrow model so that it combines these two modes of technological progress. I will assume that there is an erratic stream of innovations, each of which, when it occurs, permits a major increase in productivity. For my purposes these can be treated as exogenous. All I mean is that I am a dyed-in-the-wool macroeconomist. I am primarily interested in the relation between technological change and aggregative growth; the economics of the research sector is a secondary matter. But the formulation I want to suggest is one that would invite any do-it-yourself endogenizer to add links in the other direction, from the economic environment to the rate of innovation.

Going on at the same time is a process of continuous learning by doing, modeled in much the way that Arrow did it in 1962, and thus tied to gross investment. The main difference is that I will suppose that learning by doing would soon exhaust itself were it not for the intermittent occurrence of major innovations.

My hope is that this sort of model captures a bit more than either of its components, but that remains to be seen. There is also something to be said for learning by experimenting.

2 «»

COMBINING
INNOVATION AND
CONTINUOUS
IMPROVEMENT

There is a folk theory about the pathway from scientific research to increased productivity. Pure scientists make discoveries about the fundamental nature of things. Applied scientists reduce these basic discoveries to more mundane characteristics of more or less familiar objects. Even more applied scientists and engineers use this knowledge to design new products and invent new ways of making them at reasonable cost. Engineers translate all this into workable production plans, perhaps designing new sorts of capital equipment as part of the process. Finally, all this intellectual effort gets translated into higher productivity, either because the new goods are more valuable than the alternatives they replace or because production can achieve a higher level of efficiency— or both reasons may apply. This "linear" model of the chain of events leading to technological progress seems to lie behind most public discussion of the health of the science-technology system and of the role of government in supporting and improving it.

The linear model is not all wrong. For instance, there is a difference between research that is motivated by questions internal to a science (resolving anomalies, accounting for persistent but unexplained empirical regularities, that sort of thing) and research that is motivated by questions of immediate application outside of science (like creating an abrasive that will function in specified extreme circumstances or designing a sensor that will deploy an automobile air bag when it is needed and not when it is not). Economists will easily recognize similar distinctions in their own work.

Nevertheless close observers of the people, institutions, and processes that create and use new technology think that the linear model is highly misleading. It is much too one-directional, for instance. Quite a lot of new technology, both on the product side and the process side, originates with the consumer rather than the producer and thus moves upstream rather than downstream. But I am more interested in yet another deficiency of the folk model, the one I mentioned at the end of the last chapter. A major component of on-going productivity increase has little or nothing to do with the R&D complex at all. And this is no mere curiosity. The routine continuous improvement of products and processes is arguably the most important source of increased productivity in mature industries. In those industries it is what distinguishes successful firms and nations from unsuccessful firms and nations.

My working assumption is that continuous improvement is what learning by doing is actually about. The flow of gross investment does not usually create anything worth calling new technology. It does, however, generate useful know-how, improvements in plant layout and materials handling, economies in the number and location of fasteners, time-and-effort-saving changes in the allocation of jobs to people, and a hundred other ways to improve quality and reduce waste in the production of more or less unchanged products by more or less unchanged methods. That is almost certainly what was going on in airframe production, not technological change proper. Of course it may be cumulated production rather than cumulated gross investment that best measures the opportunity for learning by doing. For the sake of continuity I will stick with Arrow's original formulation. The general lessons will be the same either way.

The identification of learning by doing with continuous improvement does suggest one significant change in the way the process is modeled. Within the framework of a given technology, the scope for increased productivity is very likely limited. In the specific context of the Arrow model, learning by doing cannot hope to reduce the labor requirement for manning a machine arbitrarily close to zero; but that is what is required by the classical learning-curve formulation that sets the labor input associated with a unit of investment at bG^{-n} where G is the cumulative gross investment at the time that the machine in question was built. So I shall modify the model to say that the corresponding labor input is $B + bG^{-n}$. If we hold to Arrow's assumption that every unit of investment generates a rate of output equal to a whenever it is used, the implication is that learning by doing can increase labor productivity only to the limiting value a/B within the framework of a given technology. The original model had $B = 0$, so an unending story of economic growth could be told in these terms. That is not possible in my current interpretation; indeed that is the point of it.

This way of looking at bounded learning by doing is my own, but I do want to say that the general concept of bounded learning by doing has been explored by Alwyn Young in a couple of very ingenious papers. Young's interest is primarily in the activity of creating new technology. He models deliberate technological progress as the creation of new and newer goods along a spectrum of possibilities. Once a brand-new good has been invented, there is a process of cost reduction through an automatic learning by doing keyed to cumulative production. This process is inherently limited, however. Eventually it comes to an end, and sooner or later the formerly newest good is superseded by others and passes into obsolescence, to be seen no more. Growth takes the form of increasing consumer satisfaction through the variety and modernity of the menu of goods currently produced. I can see the charm of this approach (reminiscent of the quality ladders of Grossman and Helpman). But I am hooked on aggregative growth via rising productivity of labor, so I will stick to simpler and more traditional metaphors.

Unfortunately this harmless-looking constant B makes the model harder to deal with explicitly—by which I mean only that one cannot generally write down an equation as simple as (3) in the first chapter; there is no deeper conceptual problem. From now on, therefore, I shall deal only with the special case $n = 1/2$ because that does allow explicit solutions, thanks to the quadratic formula. It would be surprising if this case were not fairly representative of other values of n as long as they are strictly between 0 and 1. It is usually easy to see what qualitative difference it would make if n were a little smaller or a little larger.

For completeness I will write down the modified Arrow model as I did before. Full employment requires that the margin of obsolescence be placed just to exhaust the supply of labor:

(1) $$L = \int_{G'}^{G} (B + bg^{-1/2})\, dg \,.$$

The next equation is unchanged. Aggregate output is a multiple of the amount of past gross investment still in use:

(2) $$x = a(G - G').$$

With $n = 1/2$, (1) can be solved for G'—this is where the quadratic formula helps out—and the result substituted in (2) to get a rather more complicated representation of the not-quite-production-function of the previous lecture:

(3) $$x = a\left(d\sqrt{\frac{d^2}{4} + G + d\sqrt{G} - \frac{L}{B}} - d\sqrt{G} - \frac{d^2}{2} + \frac{L}{B}\right)$$

where $d = 2b/B$.

It almost looks, from (3), as if the aggregate output producible from a given L were unbounded, contrary to what I said earlier. That turns out not to be so, however, when account is taken of required inequalities. Indeed it is obvious from (1) that $B(G - G') < L$ and thus, from (2), that $x < aL/B$ as common sense insists. So this version of equation (3) cannot be the basis for a model of economic growth if we mean by that a story in which output per worker grows without bound. That is the very point this modified model was created to illustrate. "Continuous improvement" is not the appropriate foundation for unbounded growth. No matter how long the Second World War had lasted, the number of man-hours needed to fabricate the airframe for a B-17 could not have been diminished to negligibility without some technological breakthrough. Bounded learning by doing is a lot like Old Growth Theory without exogenous technological progress. Output can grow ultimately only as fast as employment. In fact, given the fixed-proportions nature of the underlying technology, the model comes more and more to resemble the Harrod-Domar construction.

I am going to stay with the fixed coefficients, but I am also going to reintroduce an exogenous source of technological progress distinct from continuous improvement or learning by doing. The exogeneity is not a matter of principle with me. Everyone knows that there is an important endogenous element to the process of technological innovation. We can see the relevant decisions being made all around us. Candor requires me to say that I suspect there is an additional irreducible element in innovation that, if not "truly" exogenous, whatever that means, is at least not to be fully explained by the calculus of expected profit. In any case, the inner character of technological progress is not part of my intellectual program. I will model innovation in a way that easily allows the grafting on of any coherent theory of the innovation process. The particular device I shall use is very like one in the important paper of Philippe Aghion and Peter Howitt. In that paper they do endogenize what I shall leave exogenous. They find appropriate New Growth Theory implications, but they also leave behind some residual feeling of arbitrariness.

What I shall do is to assume that there is an irregular stream of innovations. Each time an innovation occurs, the lower bound B is reduced by a factor $q < 1$. Thus, after k innovations have occurred—not the same thing as the passage of a particular interval of time—the current value of B is $q^k B_0$, where B_0 is a given "initial" value. Thus I am tacitly treating q, which measures the "size" of an innovation, as a constant; one innovation is as important as another. That is a simplification. It would make sense to imagine that, once an innovation has occurred, its size q is drawn from a fixed frequency distribution on the unit interval. The natural presumption would be that very small values of q—that is, very "large" innovations—are very rare, while values of q near one are the most common. With some luck and low cunning it might be possible to carry out that program; it could certainly be embodied in Monte Carlo exercises. For my purposes, however, it is enough to work with innovations all of the same size.

As for the occurrence of innovations, the simplest story is that they form a Poisson process with arrival rate m. That is to say, there is probability mh that an innovation occurs in any very short time interval of length h and probability $1 - mh$ that nothing happens. Anyone with a theory about the innovative process itself could let the arrival rate m be a function of economic variables. That, of course, is what the endogenous-innovation branch of the New Growth Theory does. I wish them well; but if I sound skeptical, it is because I am. There is a different sort of generalization that could be tried here, and I am rather more curious about how it would work. The Poisson process, of course, assumes that discoveries of innovations in any pair of nonoverlapping intervals of time are statistically independent events. It sounds truer to life to say that, although some discoveries are isolated, others open up a whole field and make a further cluster of innovations more likely. To describe that would require a more complicated stochastic process, but it would yield a much wider range of possible histories.

There is another modeling choice to be made, and there too I want to take the easy way out. Think about the situation immediately after the arrival of an innovation. To avoid distracting complexity, imagine that it has been so long since the previous innovation that all of the capital actually in use represents gross investment that took place after the occurrence of the immediately previous innovation. Now I want to compare the first unit of investment under the new technology with the last unit of investment under the old technology. Both yield the same output, namely *a*. How about the labor requirements? There is a discrete saving of labor under the new technology, the difference being $(q^k - q^{k+1})B_0$ if the previous and current innovations are the *k*th and $(k + 1)$st in the sequence. The question is about the learning-by-doing part: does it start over, applying only to investment performed under the new technology, or does previous learning carry over unimpaired to the new technology?

In the first case initial production costs might well be higher using the new technology than using the old. Presumably, firms would invest in the new technology because they believe that it will be ultimately profitable to do so; learning by doing will allow adequate cost savings to be realized in the future, although this expectation could prove false if the next innovation were to occur too soon. In the second case there is no problem. Previous learning carries over and initial costs with the new technology are lower by the full saving achieved through the innovation. It is always immediately advantageous to invest in the latest technology. And costs will fall further as learning by doing proceeds. I will adopt the second assumption, that learning is generalized know-how and carries over unimpaired to later generations of technologies, because it is obviously simpler. Even more complicated mixed cases are no doubt possible and perhaps workable. They may be more interesting to the close student of innovation, but that is not my goal.

So the labor required to operate a unit of investment in the $(k + 1)$st generation technology is $q^{k+1}B_0 + bG^{-1/2}$ where *G* is cumulated gross investment since the beginning of the whole story. Initially, the capacity actually in use will include investment embodying the *k*th, $(k - 1)$st, and perhaps earlier generations of technology. In the full-employment version of the model, equation (1) has to be modified in the obvious way to represent a sum over successively older generations of technology. Then, of course, there is no hope of a neat formula for (3). The interval from G' to G is broken up into subintervals, each corresponding to a given generation, with B rising discontinuously by the factor q^{-1} as one generation gives way to an older one until the available labor is all employed. That determines the margin of obsolescence, and that, in turn, determines the real wage, more exactly the perfectly competitive real wage.

If the unit of investment at the margin of obsolescence belongs to generation i and has serial number G', then the product wage must be $[a/(q^i B_0 + b G'^{-1/2})]$ because that will leave zero rent at the extensive margin. As time and gross investment go on, always taking advantage of the most recent technology, the margin of obsolescence moves smoothly through higher values of G'. The product wage increases smoothly by virtue of past learning by doing; but it takes occasional jumps when a whole generation of investment slips over the line into disuse and the marginally obsolescent unit of investment comes to embody the next most recent generation of technology.

It is easy to see how rents or profits are determined as a residual after wage payments on the supramarginal units of gross investment, so I do not need to verbalize the details. It appears that rapid innovation is good for rents in the following special sense: if the most recent innovation had occurred a bit sooner, *but the path of gross investment were unchanged*, then the full-employment wage would actually have been lower and the total of rents would have been higher. Eventually wages gain too from a faster pace of innovation. The total of incomes and their distribution between wages and rents are complicated resultants of the rate and timing of innovation, the rate and timing of gross investment, and the intensity of learning by doing. Given the complexity and uncertainty of this process, it is no wonder that business decisions about research and development spending tend to be made according to reasonable-sounding rules of thumb or by imitation of others.

In this model, the labor requirement per unit of output —the reciprocal of productivity—is the sum of two components. The continuous-improvement component is deterministic, given the time path of gross investment. The innovation component is a species of one-way random walk with logarithmically equal steps. If we look at productivity in the newest plants, the continuous-improvement component provides a smoothly rising concave time path, punctuated at irregular intervals by jumps upward as the newest plants come to represent later and later generations of technology. The size of these innovational steps can vary. If one takes the specifics of the model more literally than they deserve, then one can say that the innovational jumps become approximately equi-proportional jumps in the very long run, as the cumulated volume of gross investment gets very large. But I do not approve of going that far.

This scalloped pattern refers only to productivity at the technological frontier. For the economy as a whole, labor productivity has to be averaged over the units of gross investment currently in use and representing several generations of technology. There is nothing indeterminate or obscure about this. Nevertheless, the trend of productivity depends in a complex way on the timing of successive innovations and on the pace of investment during the random intervals within which a particular generation of technology is at the frontier. The path of gross investment plays a dual role in this process. It provides the weight attached to each technological generation in the economywide average level of productivity. It is also the major factor in determining the location of the margin of obsolescence separating viable from nonviable technologies.

The overall productivity trend will represent both true innovation and learning by doing. Innovations will bulk larger the faster they come and the larger they are (the larger is m and the smaller is q). Learning by doing will bulk larger the more rapid the pace of investment and the greater the intensity of learning (the faster the growth of G and the larger is n). Part of the lesson of this model is that we have no right to expect any statement more sweeping than that.

I would like to pursue this notion further by considering steady states. The typical paper or talk on growth theory would have discussed steady states long before this. A loose definition will do: a steady state is a solution of the model in which the important ratios—per capita quantities, for instance—are either constant or perhaps growing exponentially. Most of growth theory is about steady states: their existence, their properties as attractors, the determinants of those ratios and rates of growth. That was certainly true of Arrow's 1962 paper, as I pointed out in the first chapter. This focus on steady states has led to considerable misunderstanding of the part they play. For instance, neoclassical theory is sometimes criticized for being excessively and unrealistically dependent on the analysis of steady states.

The first thing that needs to be said is that a focus on steady states was once thought to be empirically right. Nicholas Kaldor had described half a dozen "stylized facts" of economic growth: a trendless capital-output ratio, trendless factor shares, increasing productivity and real wages, and so on. These amounted to a recipe for steady-state growth. A model with a stable steady state was, then, just what the doctor ordered. This impulse was undoubtedly reinforced by the cleanness with which an analysis of steady states can be carried out. It is only necessary to calculate how changes in important parameters affect a small number of ratios and an even smaller number of rates of growth. I still referee papers that follow this pattern faithfully. The combination of relevance and convenience is hard to beat.

The capacity to accommodate a stable steady state does not come free. Some special assumptions are required. Constant returns to scale is not among them, although the literature sometimes seems to suggest otherwise. The most important assumption is the requirement that technological progress, however it arises, should be labor augmenting in character. Quite analogously, if there are increasing or decreasing returns to scale, they must affect production in a special labor-enhancing way. These special assumptions are not required by the basic theoretical model. Their only function is to allow the model to evolve into an exponentially growing steady state. If we can do without steady states, we can do without these special assumptions. Should we? I think the correct answer is, if and only if the facts suggest that steady-state growth is a poor description of long macroeconomic time series. In the modern world of cheap computation, it is a simple matter to work out numerically the general answers to the questions that could be answered even more simply by the comparison of steady states.

Now I can explain why I have not yet looked at the steady state of the extended learning-by-doing model that I have been developing so far. The answer is that it does not have any. It is not hard to see why an exponential steady state is impossible. By design, bounded learning by doing cannot induce an unbounded growth of productivity. So steady-state growth cannot arise from that source. The discrete-innovation process is obviously not a possible source of steady growth in the literal sense, because innovations occur at random. That is a trivial remark, however. In the appropriate statistical sense, the Poisson process generating innovations, taken by itself, does have steady-state capability: the logarithm of output per worker follows a random walk with drift. (I will return to that point in a moment.) The problem is that the productivity-increasing effect of innovations is mixed up with the productivity-increasing effect coming from gross investment and continuous improvement. Since they happen at intrinsically different rates, they cannot add up to simple exponential growth, at least not exactly.

They can do so in an uninteresting limited sense. When enough investment has gone by so that the pure Arrow-like part of labor input, the part given by bG^{-n}, is essentially zero, then all that is left is the innovation component, and that can follow a stochastic steady state. I find that uninteresting, because no simple model should be taken that literally and pushed to the end of its tether. There is a symmetrically uninteresting case: if innovation occurs fast enough to reduce that part of labor input, the part given by $q^k B_0$, essentially to zero, then the model can approach the steady state analyzed by Arrow. In my mental algebra, uninteresting + uninteresting = uninteresting.

With all that in mind, it is still possible to pick up some crude conclusions about the growth of productivity, looking always at the frontier technology, even as it changes from time to time. To estimate the contribution of learning by doing, one needs a figure for the growth rate of *cumulated* gross investment. This will be less than the growth rate of investment itself if investment growth has been accelerating and will exceed the investment growth rate if investment has been decelerating. Even when no steady state is possible, it may be a reasonable benchmark to suppose the two to be approximately equal. If that common growth rate is r, then continuous improvement is lowering labor input at rate nr. That is not quite true, but I do not know any easy way to say it precisely. Labor input per unit of output is $B + bG^{-n}$ and the second term is falling at the rate nr. The next step is to look closely at B.

The discrete-innovation component falls by the factor q whenever an innovation occurs. The time between innovations is a random variable, known to follow an exponential distribution. If the arrival rate is m, the average time between innovations is $1/m$; if the probability of an innovation in any year is $1/5$ then on average an innovation occurs every five years, sometimes sooner, sometimes later. If q were, say, 0.9, that is to say if an innovation reduces labor requirements per unit of output by 10 percent (but only in newly built factories embodying the new technology), it would be fair to say that labor input per unit of output at the frontier is falling at an average rate of 2 percent a year, or more generally at the rate $m(1 - q)$.

The upshot is that labor input per unit of output is the sum of two components, one falling at the annual rate nr and the other at the annual rate $m(1 - q)$. The proportional rate at which the sum decreases is a weighted average of the two component rates, the weights being the relative sizes of the two components themselves ($q^k B_0$ and bG^{-n}). Keep in mind that the weights will be changing through time, as will the rate of growth of cumulated gross investment. It is pretty clear why no exponential steady state exists, and I hope it is clear why that does not matter. The model itself is quite determinate as soon as an investment rule is specified; a constant fraction of output will do nicely, but so will many alternatives.

Given such a rule, the model permits a calculation of intermediate-run growth rates. (I use that phrase to warn once more against pushing the story further than it will go, to the point where one of the components of growth dominates the other.) The interesting questions then concern the qualitative effects of parametric changes in the various characteristics that are featured in the model: the rate of investment, the intensity of learning by doing, the arrival rate of innovations, the size of innovations, and the inherited relative importance of the two processes that go to increase productivity. Without the convenient simplification of the steady state, it is harder to make those comparisons with pencil and paper. Maybe something can be done that way but, in any case, computer simulations could take care of the rest.

Since the focus has to be on intermediate-run growth rates, it is natural to say something about their variability. I will continue to talk in terms of labor input per unit of output, the reciprocal of productivity, because that is easier. As I have told the story, continuous improvement and discrete innovation should be statistically independent, so the variance of their sum is just the sum of separate variances. (That, too, is only an arbitrary simplification; if I had a good story, it would be interesting to imagine some positive correlation between the two processes.) The learning-by-doing component has no explicitly random character; but it seems harmless to say that the variability of that component will be large or small according as the growth rate of cumulated gross investment exhibits large or small fluctuations. That in turn will depend on the variability of the annual rate of investment, though not in any simple way. Perhaps it is enough to say that irregular growth of whatever it is that carries the continuous-improvement process will lead to irregular productivity increase from that source.

The discrete-innovation process does have a random character, and that leads me to a confession. A moment ago I argued that the average rate of productivity growth from this source is the product of the arrival rate of innovations (m) and the size of each innovation ($1 - q$). That was not quite right. What I actually calculated was the growth of productivity per unit time if the interval between innovations were at its mean length. The difference between that quantity and the average growth rate arises because the two are connected nonlinearly. It is possible to go directly to the average productivity growth rate using the fact that the number of innovations in any time interval of length T follows a Poisson distribution with mean mT. I cheated in the interest of an uncluttered exposition; but now I think I had better do the calculation properly.

Let us focus on some time interval of length T, say between t_0 and $t_0 + T$. If x innovations occur during that stretch of time, the proportional change in B can be approximated by the change in the natural logarithm of B between t_0 and $t_0 + T$, which easily turns out to be $x \ln q$. Converting this into a rate per unit time yields $x T^{-1} \ln q$ as the random rate at which labor requirements fall during that stretch of time. The expected value of this quantity is $m \ln q$, and (minus) that is approximately the mean rate of growth of productivity. (To relate this to my earlier trick, notice that $\ln q = \ln [1 - (1 - q)]$ and that in turn is approximately $-(1 - q)$.) Since the variance of x is mT, by the standard property of the Poisson distribution, it follows at once that the variance of the rate of growth is mT^{-1} $(\ln q)^2$. Using the earlier approximation again, the measure of variability we are looking for is about $m(1-q)^2/T$. This is large if innovations are large and frequent.

The details are unimportant. I only mean to illustrate that a model like this gives one a grip on intermediate-run rates of growth, their average, and their variability. Keep in mind that this characterization of productivity growth describes only what is going on in the frontier technology. Aggregation over the collection of technologies still in use is a computational matter, not something to be worked out in general. One has to decide for oneself whether the narrative advantages of abandoning steady-states outweigh the extra hassle. My feeling is that they do, provided one has already acquired a lot of experience with models that allow steady states.

In summary, then, the productivity growth rate will be more variable the more irregular the pace of investment, the larger the intensity of learning by doing (n), the larger the individual innovation ($1-q$), and the larger the arrival rate (m).

I have neither the time nor the inclination to push this sort of model any further. In a moment I will say what I think I have learned by doing the exercise. There is need, however, for a few words about the least convincing aspect of this setup. To my mind, that is the assumption that learning by doing is carried by cumulative investments since "the beginning of time." (Others might prefer to nominate the assumption that successive innovations are independent of one another, instead of forming clusters that facilitate and support each other. In some moods I might agree; but I think of that assumption as a technical simplification, to be got rid of as soon as one sees how.)

It would seem more natural, as I remarked earlier, to imagine that the learning process starts over again each time that a discrete innovation occurs. The truth is no doubt intermediate: some previous learning carries over and some does not. But it is enough to talk about the extreme cases. My main reason for choosing the less likely extreme was not that it is notationally simpler, although it is, but something more formal, maybe excessively formal.

If learning starts over with each new technology, then costs may be higher in the early stages of a new technology than they would be for users of an older technology that is already well broken in. It is still easy to understand that a producer might invest in the latest technology and swallow some early competitive disadvantage, expecting to make up for it down the road when costs have fallen. After all, that is the way learning curves are used, to project costs as experience accumulates. In order for a new technology to be economically viable, some inequalities will have to be satisfied. For instance, if the arrival rate of innovations is very high, the expected life span of old technologies will be correspondingly short. There will be less time to amortize the early cost disadvantage. I did not want to worry about those requirements. Maybe the better part of wisdom is not to worry about such formalities.

Would it make any difference if continuous improvement were handled in this alternative way? Not in any fundamental way, I suspect. The immediate increase in productivity after an innovation would be smaller because of the offset coming from this sort of anti-learning. But labor requirements per unit of output would fall a bit faster during the life span of an innovation (and therefore productivity would rise faster) because the weight of the learning-by-doing component of productivity gain would be larger than under the other dispensation. (Algebraically, if t_k is the date of the tth innovation and $t_{k+1} > t > t_k$, then obviously $[G(t) - G(t_k)]^{-n} > G(t)^{-n}$.)

But the general look of a time series generated by this model would not change qualitatively.

My main goal in these lectures has been to pay the best kind of compliment to Kenneth Arrow by showing that a 30-something-year-old work of his is still alive and well and living in the mainstream. In the course of doing so I hope to have planted a thought: that the learning-by-doing model makes even more sense when it is applied to the process of continuous improvement than in its initial incarnation as a vehicle for technological progress. This gives me an opportunity to point a moral. Continuous improvement is an important contributor to industrial performance. It has been neglected, in favor of the more glamorous idea of discrete innovation, by both American economics and American industry. Guess which is more important.

Last, and quite possibly least, I have used this excursion as the occasion for some sidelong glances at the new and the old in growth theory. My tentative conclusion has been that the value of New Growth Theory does not lie in its more or less gratuitous adoption of just those assumptions that make long-run steady-state growth rates easy to change by doing a little more of this or a little less of that. On that score, I am inclined to think, Old Growth Theory is theoretically more robust and empirically more plausible. The real contribution of the New Growth Theory is to turn the theoretical spotlight on the process that generates technological progress, part endogenous, part exogenous, part intended and expectable, part accidental and surprising. There is a body of historical and institutional study of this process, and there is plenty of industrial experience. Maybe the time is ripe for an analytical killing. I think Kenneth and I will leave it to others.

3 «»

VARIATIONS AND
SIMULATIONS

In the preceding chapter I sketched a model that combines learning by doing (or "continuous improvement") with a separate stochastic process of discrete innovations. Learning by doing leads to a fairly smooth reduction in labor required per unit of output, tied to the rate of gross investment in new capital equipment. Innovations arrive at random; when one of them happens, the labor requirement takes a jump downward. (This is not a model of research and development, although it could be converted into one.)

This model, simple as it is, does not lend itself to self-contained solution. That is not surprising. Even the Arrow model, as described in the first chapter, is not easy to deal with in detail, except in steady state. The extended model does not have a steady state, so that way of looking at it is foreclosed.

The natural next step, then, is Monte Carlo simulation of the extended model, and this chapter will report some results along that line. Once numerical simulation becomes the research tool, it is possible to add some further generality in small ways. I have taken advantage of that freedom in ways that will be described as they become relevant.

The basic model is given by equations (1) and (2) in the last chapter, with the further specification that $B = B_0 q^k$, where B_0 and q are constants and k is the number of events recorded up to now by a Poisson process with arrival rate m, also a constant. The quantity to be tracked in repeated simulations is the level of productivity (output per unit of labor) *using capital of the most recent vintage*. In the notation used in the previous chapter, this quantity is $a[bG^{-n} + B_0 q^k]^{-1}$. There is no loss of generality in setting B_0 and a equal to 1, and I have done so. Thus productivity refers to the quantity $[bG^{-n} + q^k]^{-1}$ in what follows. Varying the parameter b amounts to varying the importance of continuous improvement as compared with discrete innovation. Recording overall productivity would require averaging over all vintages of capital in use at each instant of time. I have not taken this last step, in the belief that the special character of this model would be more clearly seen in the evolution of "best-practice" productivity.

In a complete growth model, cumulative gross investment up to time t—that is, $G(t)$—would be endogenous, of course, determined by the time path of output and the rule adopted for allocating output between consumption and investment. Instead, and again because I am interested primarily in the particularity of this model of technical change, I have simply chosen the path of $G(t)$ exogenously. To begin with, I set $G_t = G_{t-1} + x_t{}^* (1 + r)^t$, where x_t are independent normally distributed variables with mean 1 and given standard deviation, and r is a number like 0.03. In other words, gross investment grows like a (proportionally) randomly disturbed geometric series. In fact, during the first set of experimental runs, G exhibited something very like smooth geometric growth.

To try the model on for size, so to speak, I show in Figures 1a and 1b some results from 100 runs, each of 50 periods, with parameters $b = 1$, $n = 0.33$, $m = 0.2$, and $q = 0.95$. That is, learning by doing occurs with the classical one-third power, an innovation occurs once every five years on average, and each innovation raises productivity by 5 percent. Figure 1a shows a handful of sample runs. Figure 1b shows the run in which productivity grew fastest, the one in which productivity grew slowest, the pointwise average of all 100 runs, with a one-standard-deviation band on either side of the average.

The first 10 or 15 periods should probably be ignored, because the effect of initial conditions is being shaken off. By the end of 50 periods, the fastest run has achieved a productivity level more than half again as high as the slowest run. The average run, which is quite smooth, of course, has achieved a productivity level of about 1.25 after 50 periods. The standard deviation is about 0.1, so a two-standard-deviation range would be fairly large. I chose this set of parameters because the sample trajectories seemed (to me) to show about the right degree of lumpiness along the productivity path. Obviously it is no trick to produce other characteristics. Productivity growth would be less regular if q or b were smaller, or m smaller, or G less smooth. Productivity growth would be speeded up if m were larger, q smaller, and r (the rate of growth of investment) larger. Figures 2a and 2b are like 1a and 1b except that b has been increased from 1 to 2. This gives more weight to the smoother continuous-improvement process, which both smooths the productivity trajectories a bit and reduces the variability a bit. I conclude from this only that the model is fairly flexible. It could clearly be calibrated to give the "right" rate of growth and degree of smoothness of the productivity path.

Figures 3a and 3b are introduced for later comparisons. In

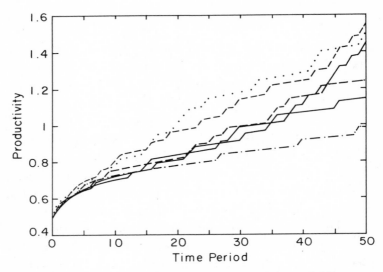

FIGURE IA. Sample runs ($b = 1, n = 0.33, m = 0.2, q = 0.95$)

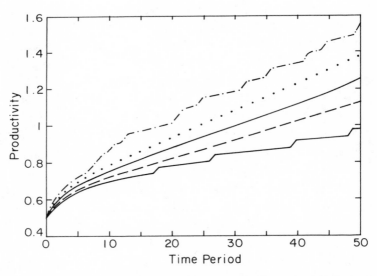

FIGURE IB. Maximum, minimum, average, and standard deviation of multiple runs ($b = 1, n = 0.33, m = 0.2, q = 0.95$)

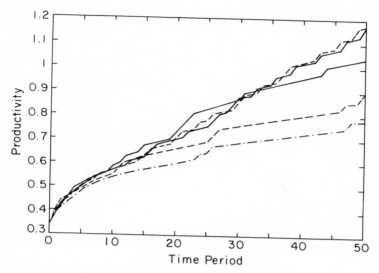

FIGURE 2A. Sample runs ($b = 2$, $n = 0.33$, $m = 0.2$, $q = 0.95$)

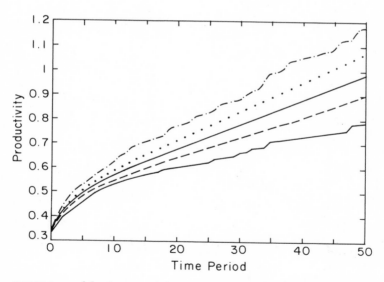

FIGURE 2B. Maximum, minimum, average, and standard deviation of multiple runs ($b = 2$, $n = 0.33$, $m = 0.2$, $q = 0.95$)

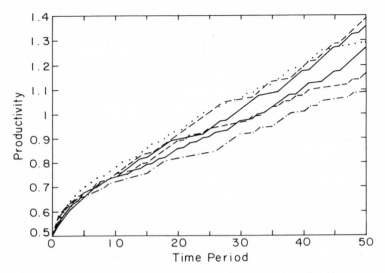

FIGURE 3A. Sample runs ($b = 1$, $n = 0.33$, $m = 0.5$, $q = 0.98$)

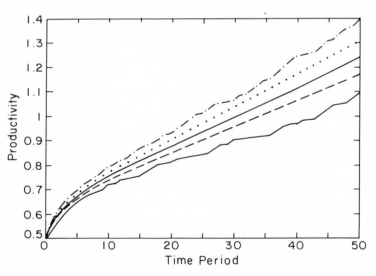

FIGURE 3B. Maximum, minimum, average, and standard deviation of multiple runs ($b = 1$, $n = 0.33$, $m = 0.5$, $q = 0.98$)

them, I go back to $b = 1$ and leave $n = 0.33$, but now $m = 0.5$ and $q = 0.98$. The product $m(1 - q)$ is unchanged, but now innovations occur more often and each one is smaller. The result is to smooth the trajectories, whether enough or too much I leave to others.

Now I want to consider a slight generalization. I have so far assumed that every innovation is the same "size." That is, each innovation reduces the labor requirement per unit of output by the same fraction, namely $(1 - q)$. In Figures 1a and 1b as in 2a and 2b, $q = 0.95$. Now I will assume that, whenever an innovation occurs, the value of q is drawn from a fixed probability distribution, so some innovations are more important than others. Here I allow q to take on the values 1.0, 0.98, 0.95, and 0.90 with probabilities 0.1, 0.2, 0.5, and 0.2 respectively. The expected value of q is 0.951, or essentially its earlier constant value. Since $1 - q = 0$ occurs with probability 0.1, one in ten innovations turns out to be a dud. Essentially, then, allowing a random q is just another source of variability in the period-to-period growth of productivity. As Figures 4a and 4b show, that is just about what happens. The spread of trajectories is a little wider, but not much. (Of course, it would be possible to allow a much wider range of values of q if that were desired.) In these last diagrams, $b = 1$ and $m = 0.2$.

To provide one more bit of experience with this model, I reproduce in Figures 5a and 5b the results with a slightly different collection of parameters. Now an innovation occurs about every second period ($m = 0.5$), but they are rather small ($q = 0.98$, so an innovation creates a 2 percent jump in productivity). The learning-by-doing exponent (n) is increased from 0.33 to 0.5, so continuous improvement is somewhat more sensitive to investment. And, finally, the investment path

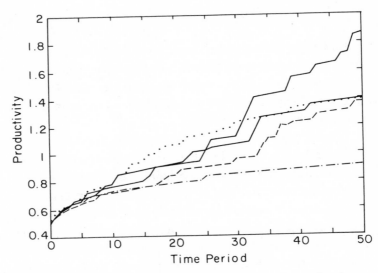

FIGURE 4A. Sample runs ($b = 1$, $n = 0.33$, $m = 0.2$, q random)

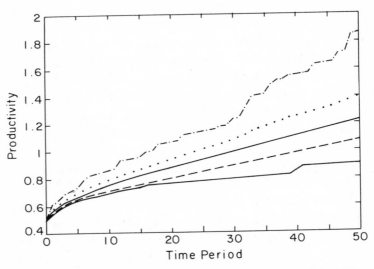

FIGURE 4B. Maximum, minimum, average, and standard deviation of multiple runs ($b = 1$, $n = 0.33$, $m = 0.2$, q random)

is made slightly more irregular; the path of $G(t)$, i.e., cumulative gross investment, is shown in Figure 5c. These trajectories look "realistic" to me. I note that this setup yields a somewhat smaller standard deviation around the average productivity path.

Now I try a more significant conceptual departure from the basic model. Up to now, the arrival rate in the innovation process has been a constant. That might be reasonable if one were thinking only of "major" inventions. More generally, one might imagine that innovations occur in clusters within which each innovation stimulates the next. This is a complicated question, not to be settled by simple algorithms. Out of curiosity, however, I try the following simple algorithm. Start with $m_0 = 0.5$. In any period t, $m_t = (1 + u) * m_{t-1}$ if an innovation occurs in period $t - 1$ and $m_t = (1 + u)^{-1} * m_{t-1}$ if no innovation occurs in period $t - 1$. Here u is a number like 0.05, 0.1, or 0.15. Anytime an innovation occurs, the chance of another innovation increases; anytime a period goes by without innovation, the probability of another innovation diminishes. The other parameters are $b = 1$, $n = 0.33$, $q = 0.98$.

The interesting representation of the results now is a plot of all 100 trajectories (each 50 time periods in length). Individual paths cannot be distinguished, but it is the ensemble that counts. Figures 6a, 6b, and 6c show the results for $u = 0.05$, 0.1, and 0.15. Figure 6a looks more or less like a dispersed collection of paths; with care, however, one can discern that there is a group of high paths with lots of innovations and a group of low paths along which innovations (i.e., jumps) are much less frequent. In Figure 6b this dichotomy is much clearer. In fact there are very few paths that end up in the middle of the pack. In Figure 6c this pattern is very clear. By $t = 20$, trajectories are separated into successful ones

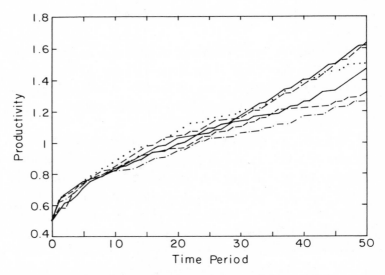

FIGURE 5A. Sample runs ($b = 1$, $n = 0.5$, $m = 0.5$, $q = 0.98$)

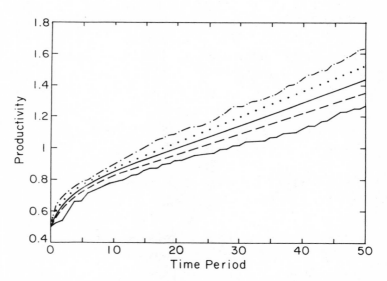

FIGURE 5B. Maximum, minimum, average, and standard deviation of multiple runs ($b = 1$, $n = 0.5$, $m = 0.5$, $q = 0.98$)

and unsuccessful ones. Early success begets later success; early failure reproduces itself as the arrival rate shrinks. During the 35 periods from $t = 15$ to $t = 50$, the successful paths roughly double their productivity while the unsuccessful ones increase their productivity by about a quarter.

The mechanism is completely transparent and far too simple. The only comment I want to make is that this sort of mechanism could provide an argument for a sort of "big push" policy on the technological side. An economy drifting with the lower pack might (maybe) be transferred into the upper pack by a deliberate campaign to increase the rate of innovation—if anyone knows how to do that.

It is easy to make small alterations in this mechanism. For instance, an asymmetry can be introduced: instead of multipliers equal to $(1 + u)$ and $(1 + u)^{-1}$ when innovations occur

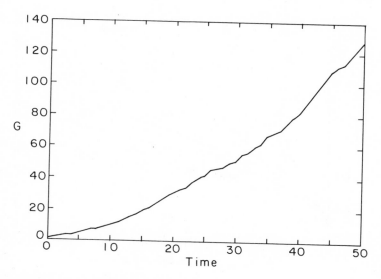

FIGURE 5C. Cumulative gross investment

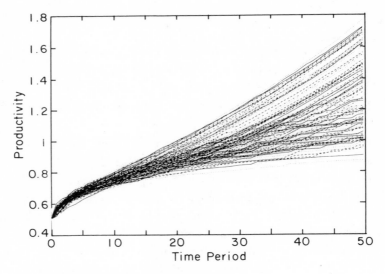

FIGURE 6A. Graph of 100 runs ($u = 0.05$)

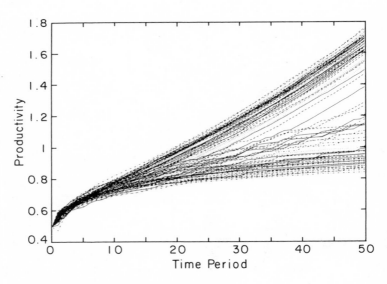

FIGURE 6B. Graph of 100 runs ($u = 0.1$)

or do not occur, the multipliers could be $(1 + u)$ and $(1 + v)^{-1}$. Alternatively, or in addition, upper and lower bounds can be placed on m_t to prevent runaway cases. I do not dwell on the results of such experiments, because they come out just as one would expect.

Although the focus in these lectures is appropriately on learning by doing, most of the variations that have been explored in these Monte Carlo experiments have been elaborations of the innovations process. I am not sure why that should be so. Most likely the possibilities have been tied down by Arrow's original and convenient formulation. There is little room for small alterations in the model itself. Variations in the parameter n have predictable consequences. Variations in b amount merely to changing the relative weight of learning by doing and more traditional innovation in the process of

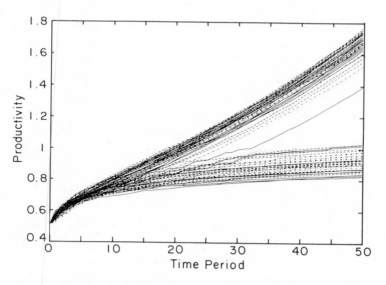

FIGURE 6C. Graph of 100 runs ($u = 0.15$)

improving productivity. That, it seems to me, is the most interesting open question: how much of what we see is continuous improvement and how much is R&D-induced technological innovation? The answer to that question would certainly be relevant to policy decisions aimed at accelerating the productivity trend. The answer is not likely to be found by looking at computer simulations of the model. But the simulations might be useful in improving the model and in figuring out a reasonable and practical empirical test. At least that is why I have thought them worth carrying out.

This train of thought is what led to the next set of experiments to be reported. One of the distinctive characteristics of the Arrow model is that it ties its special source of productivity increase to ordinary capital investment. A natural question to ask, then, is about the sensitivity of the productivity trend to the investment trend. (Reminder: this has nothing to do with the growth-theoretic question about the relation between the saving-investment share of output and the steady-state growth rate. As shown in the first chapter, the Arrow model can be Old Growth Theory or New Growth Theory, depending on whether the parameter n is less than one or exactly equal to one. The numerical solutions in this chapter all have $n < 1$.)

I get at this connection in the following way. The duration of each computer run is extended from 50 periods to 100 periods. The number of runs in each set is increased from 100 to 200, for a purely presentational reason: I include some histograms, and they look better when the sample size is as large as 200. For the first 50 periods of each run, the path of gross investment is as it was before, growing at 3 percent per period, although subject to random proportional disturbances. From period 51 to 100, however, the rate of growth of investment jumps to a higher or lower figure, and the goal is to see what this acceleration of investment does to the productivity trend. (Obviously this dodges the growth-theoretic question. The difficulty, in Old Growth Theory, is to create and sustain an acceleration of investment.)

In these simulations, the standard parameters are $b = 1$, $n = 0.33$, $m = 0.2$, q is itself random with mean 0.95. Instead of exhibiting the trajectories themselves, I reproduce histograms of "normalized" productivity at the end of the 100th time period, say. The quantity whose frequency distribution is represented in this way is the productivity level achieved by the 200 separate runs after 100 periods. ("Normalized" refers to the fact that in each case the productivity level is relative to its level at $t = 10$; this is done to attenuate the effect of initial conditions.)

Figure 7a depicts the base case in which the growth rate of investment is 3 percent per period for the whole span of 100 periods. The center of the distribution is between 2.5 and 3, and the spread is fairly wide. Figure 7b differs in that the growth rate of investment fell from 3 to 1 percent per year in period 51 and remained there until the end. To my eye, the range of the distribution has changed very little, and the mass of the distribution has shifted noticeably to the left. One clear way to see this is to compare the mass to the right of 3 and to the left of 2.5 in the two histograms. I have not shown the corresponding histogram when investment grows at 2 percent per period in the second half, but I will report that it is barely distinguishable from Figure 7a. Interestingly, Figure 7c tells a rather stronger story. The growth rate of investment is increased to 5 percent per period for the second half of the run. The result is a perceptible shift of the histogram to the right, especially visible in the pile-up of frequency in the open-ended bin at 4. The center of the distribution is somewhere around

3, maybe even a bit higher. (The intermediate case in which the investment growth rate shifts to 4 percent per period also shows a significant effect on the productivity trend.)

Is this a big response or a small one? I would rather not say, not with so simple a model. The representative productivity gain between Figure 7a and 7c is perhaps 20–25 percent over 50 periods. That is about 0.5 percent per period. If the model's unit period is taken to be a year, then accelerating the productivity trend by 0.5 percent per year is a substantial achievement. But a sustained acceleration of investment growth from 3 to 5 percent per year represents an effort probably beyond achievement. No such discussion can pretend to realism. The point is that the learning-by-doing model shows a definite sensitivity to the pace of gross investment.

It should be kept in mind that the random innovation-process is going on all the time in these simulations. So the

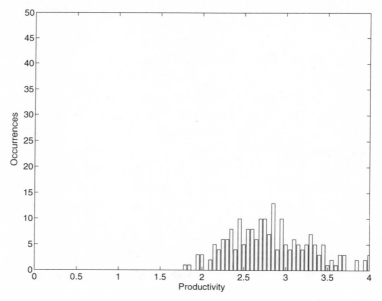

FIGURE 7A. Normalized histogram of all runs in 100th time period (*g* grows at 3 percent)

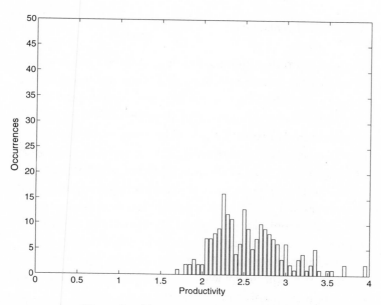

FIGURE 7B. Normalized histogram of all runs in 100th time period (*g* grows at 1 percent)

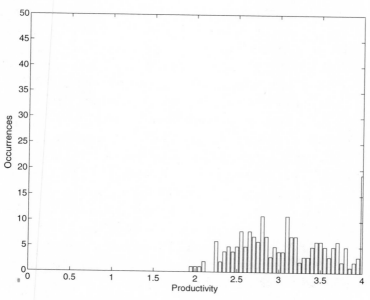

FIGURE 7C. Normalized histogram of all runs in 100th time period (*g* grows at 5 percent)

effects of learning by doing are diluted by the other source of productivity increase. Those effects would be more visible in a pure learning-by-doing model. I will report, without exhibiting the corresponding histograms, that this sensitivity to the rate of investment is enhanced by appropriate changes in the parameters of the learning-by-doing process. For instance, if b is increased to 2, so that the sheer weight of learning by doing is greater compared with exogenous innovation, or if n is increased to 0.5, so that labor requirements fall more easily with cumulative investment, the effect of accelerated investment on the final-period histograms becomes even more clearly visible.

As a last experiment with this model, I combine two of the variations already explored. I start with the version in which the arrival rate of innovations itself depends on past experience. Thus $m_0 = 0.5$, so initially the probability of an innovation in any period is one-half. Then $v = u = 0.05$; the arrival rate rises by 5 percent (of itself) in the period immediately after one in which an innovation occurs, and falls by 5 percent in the period immediately after one in which an innovation does not occur. But an upper bound of 0.8 and a lower bound of 0.2 are imposed on m_t: if the arrival rate reaches the upper (lower) bound and "wants" to go higher (lower), it is constrained to stay at the corresponding bound. Apart from this, the standard parameters are $b = 1$, $n = 0.33$, $q = 0.98$. Thus $m(1 - q)$ starts at about 0.01, the average rate of productivity growth from the innovation process.

As seen earlier, this is the sort of model in which trajectories tend to dichotomize into "successful" and "relatively unsuccessful" growth paths. This is because success in innovation breeds success in the model, and the absence of innovation makes future innovation less likely. It should be clearly understood that this model has been parameterized to exaggerate the dichotomization of trajectories. This is because the initial arrival rate is as high as 0.5. A success in the first period pushes the arrival rate to 0.525; a failure reduces it to 0.475. This is already a noticeable difference. If the initial arrival rate were 0.1, then the second-period arrival rate would be 0.105 after a success and 0.095 after a failure, not such a big difference in odds. The exaggeration is intended, of course, precisely to make the dichotomization clearly visible.

Using this model, I now try the experiment of running the model through 50 periods during which investment grows at an average rate of 3 percent per period, followed by 50 periods during which investment grows at a slower rate (1 or 2 percent per period) or a faster rate (4 or 5 percent per period). For comparison, there is one set of runs in which investment continues to grow at 3 percent per period. There are then five sets of 100-period runs, each set consisting of 200 runs. There are two stochastic elements in each run: the evolution of the arrival rate of innovations and the proportional disturbances to the investment series.

The results are displayed in five histograms, Figures 8 a, b, c, d, and e, corresponding to ascending rates of growth in periods 51–100. The quantity whose frequency distribution is illustrated is, for each run, the ratio of the productivity level at $t = 100$ to the level achieved at $t = 50$. The idea is to see how the acceleration of investment affects the growth of productivity, via the learning-by-doing mechanism. The first 50 periods serve the purpose of letting the model settle down in adaptation to 3 percent growth of investment, before imposing a different experience.

The first thing to say is that the dichotomization of trajectories is clearly visible in the bimodal frequency distributions.

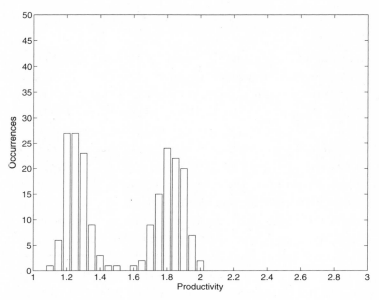

FIGURE 8A. Ratio of 100th period to 50th period (*g* grows at 1 percent)

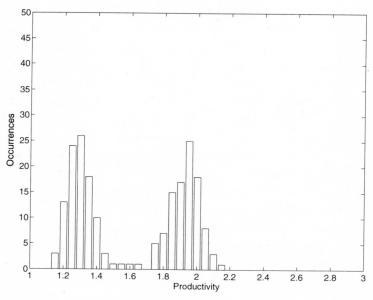

FIGURE 8B. Ratio of 100th period to 50th period (*g* grows at 2 percent)

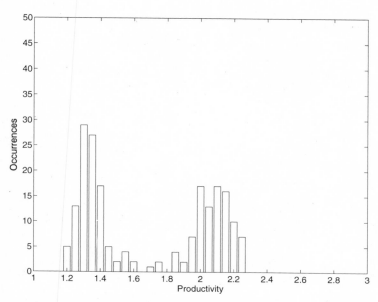

FIGURE 8C. Ratio of 100th period to 50th period (*g* grows at 3 percent)

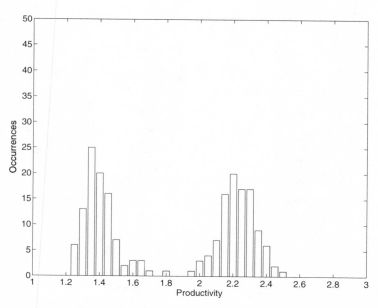

FIGURE 8D. Ratio of 100th period to 50th period (*g* grows at 4 percent)

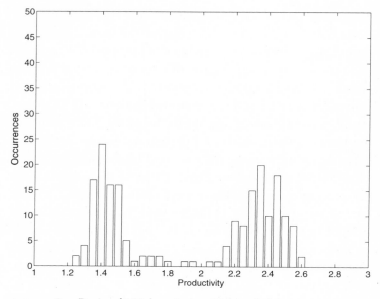

FIGURE 8E. Ratio of 100th period to 50th period (g grows at 5 percent)

As one would expect from the symmetry of the model, about half of the runs in each set fall into the upper subdistribution, and the rest into the lower. I have already explained that the model does not need to give such extreme results.

Of course, it is the differences among the histograms that show the effects of faster or slower growth of investment on productivity growth, as mediated by learning by doing. There is no alternative to looking separately at the two halves of each bimodal distribution. There is no guarantee, by the way, that trajectories that were in the upper pack at $t = 50$ are still in the upper pack at $t = 100$. In fact, there are a few crossovers, but very few, so there is no distortion in ignoring them.

Look first at the base case, shown in Figure 8c, where

the growth rate of investment remains at 3 percent during the second half of the run. The center of the lower half of the histogram is at about 1.35, and that of the upper half at about 2.1. These correspond to growth rates of about 0.6 percent and 1.5 percent per period respectively. If these measures are compared with those derived from Figure 8a, say 1.25 and 1.82, we can say something like the following. The shift of the investment growth rate from 3 percent to 1 percent per period costs the unlucky productivity trajectories about 30 percent of their 50-period growth and costs the lucky trajectories about 25 percent of theirs. (These are calculated as $(35 - 25)/35$ and $(1.10 - 0.82)/1.10$.) I do not know how to decide if this is a lot or a little; but it should be kept in mind that we are talking about a pretty drastic collapse of gross investment. Figure 8b, corresponding to 2 percent growth of investment, falls roughly midway between 8a and 8c; no surprise there.

A similar look at Figure 8e leads to symmetric conclusions. The center of the lower distribution is roughly 1.45 and that of the upper hump is, at a guess, between 2.35 and 2.4. Thus the acceleration of investment growth from 3 percent to 5 percent per period increases the 50-year gain in productivity by some 30 percent for the unlucky trajectories and some 25 percent for the group of fast trajectories. Once again Figure 8d, at 4 percent investment growth, lies between 8c and 8e. These are nontrivial payoffs, but I suppose the moral is that learning by doing shares with Old Growth Theory the characteristic that it takes a lot of investment to make a dent in productivity.

The dispersion in these histograms is striking. The difference between the lucky and unlucky packs is very large. In Figure 8c, the difference between the upper and lower centers means that the average lucky trajectory has achieved a productivity level about 55 percent higher than the average unlucky trajectory. That means about three *times* as much growth. But this difference has been deliberately magnified. Even within the lucky and unlucky packs there is a lot of dispersion. A lucky trajectory in the lucky pack has achieved a productivity level 20–25 percent higher than an unlucky trajectory in the lucky pack. This means about 50 percent more growth in 50 periods. Within the lower pack, the upper tail has productivity one-third greater than the lower tail, and the growth comparison is between a 20 percent increase and a 60 percent increase over 50 periods.

Since these are just model calculations, I draw mainly methodological conclusions from them. First, the model of learning by doing, which I interpret as being much the same thing as "continuous improvement," has had very little improvement since Arrow's time. It is worth developing, if only because it would be practically useful to be able to measure the separate contributions of continuous improvement and traditional innovation. (There's a budding oxymoron for you!) Even more important is the possibility that there are institutional changes that would foster learning by doing; it cannot be as mechanical a process as Arrow made it and as I have left it. The incentives are not necessarily the same as R&D incentives. If, as some have suggested, continuous improvement is more characteristic of mature industries and discrete innovation more characteristic of new industries, then the interaction may be interesting.

Second, I hope the sort of combined model illustrated in these lectures might be a good vehicle for endogenizing both sources of productivity gain. The arrival rate of innovations and, perhaps, the size parameter are obvious things to model. My own prejudice is to leave something to chance and/or exogeneity in both continuous improvement and discrete innovation.

Finally, these being the Arrow Lectures, I should hope they suggest how useful a good middlebrow idea can be, if you treat it right.

4 «»

POLICIES FOR ECONOMIC GROWTH

The Sturc lecture series was established to honor the memory of a man who functioned—and functioned well—in the real world. Most of the previous lecturers, maybe all of them, have had their attention firmly focused on the real world in which Ernest Sturc functioned. They have been thinkers, but thinkers whose center of gravity has been where decisions are made and actions debated and initiated.

This time the powers that be have invited a theorist to give the Sturc Lecture. A theorist is someone whose attention is riveted on a make-believe world, whose goal is to understand everything about that world. Most theorists hope that their particular make-believe world can tell us something, although obviously not everything, about the world we actually live in. The made-up world has a disadvantage. It may be an untrustworthy guide to the real world, the way a large-scale map may not tell you that the forest it shows is infested with poison ivy. But the made-up world has an advantage, too. It is possible to understand it completely. The real world is much too complicated for that.

Of course, there is only one real world but no limit to the toy worlds that economic theorists can invent. Not all of the pretend worlds are interesting or useful. Sometimes imagination runs wild. Anyone, practical person or theorist, is entitled to think that *this* toy economy has characteristics that make it a reasonable, simplified model of the real world but *that* toy economy does not. There is an art to making those distinctions, and there is more than art. Some toys look more like the real thing than others. They can never reproduce reality, but it is possible to check if they at least produce some of the right responses, like a baby doll that wets when given something to drink. Some toy worlds fail the test pretty quickly. Others survive—like the drum-beating rabbit with the flashlight battery, they're still going.

So, as J. Durante used to say, "Them's the conditions that prevail." I am here representing a lot of economists who have studied what makes toy economies grow and what governs the paths that they follow when short-run fluctuations are averaged away. My task is to tell you what we think we have learned about the mechanism of long-term economic growth, about the forces that make one economy grow robustly and another stagnate. With some success in that endeavor, we should be able to distinguish policies that favor economic growth from policies that discourage it.

In a simplified, make-believe economy the range of policies one can talk about is pretty simple too, describable only in fairly general abstract terms. You would never leave the making of economic policy to theorists because good policy has to accommodate the particularities and inhabitants of the real world. But I believe it is also a mistake to make and carry out policy for economic growth and for other goals without consulting the theorists. Why? Because practical people often pay inadequate attention to fundamental interconnections. They forget that the knee bone connected to the thigh bone, the thigh bone connected to the hip bone, and so they don't adequately praise the ways of the Lord.

Before I get on with my story, there is an important qualification to make. I mean to talk about growth, not about modernization, not about the transformation of a predominantly agricultural and handicraft economy with low and stagnant income into an industrial economy practicing a sophisticated division of labor, coordinated by a reasonably well functioning network of markets and generating high and rising incomes. The sort of theory I want to exploit already presupposes that second sort of economy and tries to understand its growth. The tools I know and can apply do not provide an answer to the other question: how do poor and primitive economies get onto that track in the first place? When those tools are pressed into service in that inappropriate way—as some economists press them—they often give questionable or foolish answers, or so I think. The make-believe economy I have in mind might perhaps be Brazil or Taiwan or Portugal with a GNP per worker in 1988 equal to one-third, give or take a couple of percentage points, of the U.S. figure of $37,608 in 1985 international prices. But I do not imagine it could be Guyana or Zimbabwe or Bangladesh whose GNP per worker is estimated (by Summers and Heston) to be between 6.5 and 8.5 percent of the U.S. level.

Even the merest beginning of Eastern Europe's transformation has made unmistakably clear how much economic development depends on the presence of the institutional and attitudinal infrastructure of a modern capitalist economy. This includes such things as a worked-out and generally accepted framework of property rights, enforcement of contracts, and a whole slew of market institutions, including financial institutions that can gather savings, evaluate loan quality, and control risk. Underlying the institutions are indispensable attitudes: toward work, toward entrepreneurship, toward the impersonality of economic activity in general. For insight into all this you would turn more naturally to Max Weber than to a modern growth theorist. I am assuming all those attitudes and institutions are already in place. The question is what determines the rate and pattern of economic growth, not what gets it started in the first place.

When we discuss economic growth, just what is it that is supposed to grow? I have nothing special to say about population growth, although it can be important. So we will be thinking about growth per capita. That still leaves it open whether it is growth of output per person in the population, or per person employed, or per hour worked, or even per unit of all factors of production, including capital and natural resources. For most purposes any one of these measures of productivity will do, so long as we are conscious of the specific choice that has been made. One would look differently on increases in national output per person that come about by increasing the length of the work week or by attracting people from school, home, or retirement into the active workforce or by "pure" increases in productivity. Generally, unless I say something to the contrary, I will mean growth of output per hour worked.

A second ambiguity is potentially more confusing. It is not a good idea to mix up economic growth and business-cycle upswings. Journalistic writing and political debate often describe any year-to-year or quarter-to-quarter increase in national output as "growth." Some increases in output come from the activation of idle capital and idle — even if employed

—labor. Sometimes, of course, the economy goes into reverse and output falls. These fluctuations are quite different from the changes that occur in the course of economic growth. They have different causes and also different consequences. They call for different policies. When I speak of economic growth, I mean to refer to increases in the *capacity* to produce output, not in production itself. Sometimes it is possible to distinguish between the *potential* output of an economy and its *actual* output. The business cycle consists in fluctuations of actual output around a given trend of potential output. The story of growth is the story of the trend of potential, and growth-oriented policy is policy aimed at affecting the potential trend.

Finally, a more subtle distinction has to do with the phrase "long run." When model-building economists talk technically about economic growth, they are usually thinking about a "steady state" or about growth that continues at a more or less steady rate for a very long time. They know it cannot go on forever, but for some interesting questions there is not much difference between "forever" and "for a long time." Now think of a quite different situation. Imagine an economy that has a constant, unchanging level of productivity. Then something happens—the invention of the computer, for instance—and productivity begins to rise. We know it will reach a new plateau and level off there. Then it will become constant again, higher than it was before but no longer changing. Such a process might take 30 years or even longer for a major invention. If you look at the annual growth rate, it will start at zero, build up to a positive value, perhaps quite suddenly, then start to fall back and reach zero again after 30 years have passed.

How shall we describe that episode? Of course, I have

just described it quite accurately. Perhaps nothing more is needed. But should we classify it as an episode of temporary growth or as something else? It is surely not a steady state, and steady-state theory should not be applied. I do not object to classifying this story as an interval of temporary growth. Such one-time gains in productivity are very valuable achievements. If growth is glamorous, then maybe it is useful propaganda to talk about a temporary burst of growth. If we do that, however, we must remember that it is not an occasion for blame when the annual growth rate starts to fall toward zero. The fall in the growth rate is not necessarily some kind of failure—it is a natural and inevitable part of the process of getting from one productivity plateau to a higher one. Achieving a new plateau is to be distinguished from achieving a higher growth rate that can be counted on for a long time. A careful vocabulary will preserve that distinction.

The modern theory of economic growth as developed in the 1950s and 1960s had implications for policy that were generally felt to be rather pessimistic. It may have been a misguided evaluation, but that is how it seemed at the time. The essential conclusion was that the long-run steady-state growth rate for a national economy could be expressed as the sum of two numbers. The first was the rate of growth of employment, measured in total hours worked. The second was described as the rate of "technological progress," but it was well understood that this had to be interpreted very broadly to include changes in the health, educational level, and motivation of workers, and changes in the efficiency with which markets allocate resources of labor and capital to production. (It was a sign of the times that use of natural resources played no role in the theory. But that was taken care of in the 1970s when the Organization of Petroleum Exporting Countries served as a reminder.) According to this scheme, growth of output per hour worked has its only permanent source in this generalized sort of technological progress.

The point may be clearer if I state it another way. We can construct a more or less complete list of all the inputs into national production, including as a species of input the level of technology achieved. Then sustained growth can be generated only by sustained growth of some or all of these inputs. Sustained growth of output per hour worked can be generated only by sustained growth of some or all of the inputs when they too are expressed per hour worked, except for the level of technology. The reason for the difference is the natural presumption that technology is not "used up" when spread over a larger number of workers or hours as ordinary inputs are.

Growth in the level of technology is exactly what is meant by technological progress. To the extent that changes in the quality of labor and in the efficiency of resource-allocation can be measured separately and included in the list of inputs, the index of technological progress can be purified of those elements and restricted to narrowly technological factors. But it is probably essential to include improvements in the organization of production as well as traditional engineering-based improvements in machine operation, process control, and materials.

The same sort of argument leads to the conclusion that sustained productivity growth can also come from growth in the stock of human capital per worker and from growth in the stock of ordinary plant and equipment per worker. It follows then that policies to accelerate growth must aim at *increasing* the sustained growth of human or physical capital. This is where the theory's pessimism enters, if that is the right name for it.

It turns out to be no easy matter to create a permanent increase in the *rate of growth* of the stock of physical capital. Suppose there are diminishing returns to capital. That is an economist's phrase, but it has an everyday meaning. Imagine piling more and more plant and equipment on a fixed base of labor and natural resources, so that production becomes steadily more capital-intensive. If the profitability of successive doses of investment gets smaller and smaller under those circumstances, then the famous law of diminishing returns applies. It turns out that there is a natural upper limit to the growth of capital per worker, and that limit is the rate of technological progress. The limit shows itself in the following way: a national economy that tries to keep its stock of capital growing any faster will find itself forced to invest a larger and larger fraction of its national product. But it cannot invest more than all of its output, except by temporary borrowing, and long before that stage the reduced profitability of investment will surely call a halt to the process of increasing capital intensity. There is no hope of accelerating growth beyond the "natural" limits for more than a relatively short time.

This is an important point, so I will put it in yet another way. An economy dissatisfied with its rate of growth might propose to do better by devoting a larger fraction of its national product to investment. If it had previously been investing about 20 percent of GNP, it might try to invest 25 percent from now on. This could be accomplished by any policy that increased the profitability of investment: by lowering taxes on business profit or by direct subsidization of private investment, accompanied perhaps by increased public investment. What the theory says, and what most economists believed (at least until very recently), is that such an increase in the national investment share would create only a temporary episode of faster growth of the sort I described earlier. The growth-promoting policy would indeed bring about an immediate acceleration of the overall growth rate, but eventually the growth rate would fall back to where it was before. The economy would be richer for having invested more; the gain would take the form of a *higher* income per worker or per person, but not a more rapidly *growing* income per person. I want to emphasize that it could be very worthwhile to exchange a higher fraction of income saved for a higher level of income. The result could be higher consumption per person, growing as before. It is only the rash demands of citizens and the even rasher promises of political candidates that make this reward seem minor compared with the impossible wish for a higher growth rate.

It appears at first obvious that whatever is true about physical capital should be true of human capital. They seem quite analogous. That may indeed be the case, and then the same proposition holds: acceleration of the permanent growth rate cannot be achieved by accelerating the growth of the stock of human capital. An attempt to do so would be frustrated by the increasing cost, in labor time and other resources, of "producing" additional human capital. But the analogy admittedly may not be so close. The accumulation of human capital appears to be much more a matter of quality than of quantity. People acquire new skills rather than more of the old skill. Of course, we speak all the time of more education or more training, but then we seem to be measuring input into the education or training process rather than what comes out of it. I am not sure about any of this; I only want to mention the possibility that the accumulation of human capital obeys rather different laws from those governing physical capital, in terms of its own production and perhaps in terms of its use in the production of goods. It is possible, then, that sustaining faster economic growth through accelerated accumulation of human capital is a feasible proposition. One should not just assume this to be so; uncertainty is not a license for optimism. It might be the prudent course to adopt the pessimistic view with respect to human capital, too.

Having said this, I should point out that the same reasoning also suggests a little uncertainty about physical capital as well. The increase of capital intensity is usually accompanied by changes in the quality of capital goods and not merely their quantity. So perhaps the presumption of diminishing returns is not so plausible even there. Economic theory tries to handle this difficulty by treating the improved quality or different character of capital goods as an aspect of technological change. When old machinery is replaced by new machinery that costs more, the higher cost is added to the "stock of capital" and the effects of its "newness" are somehow incorporated in a higher level of technology. I do not want to pretend that this is a straightforward or exact procedure. It has been much argued about. But it is an approximate way— and so far the only way—to get on with the job. If it is fair to deal with physical capital this way, the same method might be applied to human capital, to make a separation into "more" and "better." Unfortunately there is little or no experience to guide us. Even if human capital is subject to diminishing returns, its importance in the growth process offers some scope for policies that can increase the level of income permanently, even if not the growth rate.

With all these qualifications, the conclusion from postwar growth theory was that the *only* source of *sustained* acceleration of growth is somehow a faster rate of technological progress. A policy aimed at faster growth for a very long period must then be aimed at steady improvement in the level of technology that is available to apply to industrial production. Some of this can come from faster imitation of technological leaders elsewhere in the world, and some can come from faster application of known technology from laboratory to factory. But eventually it will have to come from the faster accumulation of technological knowledge.

We all know there is a chance element in the process of technological innovation. Lightning strikes. It strikes where the ground has been prepared, but it does not automatically strike just because the ground has been prepared. We all also know that the chance element is only a part of the process. The rest is deliberate, and costly. Resources have to be mobilized and spent, in the form of people and of objects. When more is spent, more is likely to be achieved, even if one cannot be sure exactly what will be achieved. So there is something for growth-oriented policy to do. Governments play a direct part in organizing and financing research and can make research more profitable for the private sector, just as with other forms of investment.

Nevertheless, we understand very little about the process of technological innovation and not much more about the process of translating new technology into higher productivity. No one doubts that spending more people and resources on innovation will produce more innovation. But the quantitative links are another matter. What would it take to raise the rate of technological progress by 1 percent per year and sustain it? Anyone who will venture an answer to that question is living dangerously. Is there a basis for policy here? I think there is. Private enterprise almost certainly invests less in research and development than society at large would and should wish. More would be better, and the payoff would certainly be in higher productivity, whose benefits are very widely diffused. But exactness in this kind of calculation is not attainable. I doubt anyone will ever be able to say accurately that this program of research and development will add *x* percent to national product per worker or that another program will add *y* percent per year to the preexisting rate of productivity increase.

I do not know whether that is a discouraging conclusion. From the economist's point of view it is. Of course, one would like to replace vagueness by precision or the hope of precision. From the point of view of the policymaker, however, it is not so discouraging. Intelligent policy can still be made — and modesty was once thought to be a virtue.

So far I have been describing what the Old Growth Theory, the growth theory of the 1950s and 1960s, had to say about policies for economic growth. Let me try to summarize, without the nuances. To do so I will go back to the idea of a trend of potential output, an index of what the economy can achieve if it operates always at some normal or desirable rate of capacity utilization or some acceptable unemployment rate. There is no harm in expressing the potential in terms of output per worker or per hour worked. The theory differentiated sharply between policies that could *lift* the potential trend curve from those that could *tilt* the curve, that is, change the rate of growth. The conclusion was that the conventional range of fiscal or regulatory policies, those aimed at increasing the rate of capital formation, or even the rate of human capital formation, could lift the potential trend but not tilt it. A sustained increase in the share of GNP invested would create only a temporary episode of accelerated growth. The payoff to a reduction in current consumption would be a permanent increase in the level of consumption beginning sometime in the future. To tilt the potential curve would require a rise in the rate of technological progress. Some policies might accomplish that goal: promotion of research and development, encouragement of entrepreneurial behavior, possibly prayer. The benefit of such policies can be very great, but the degree of their success is uncertain and probably intrinsically uncertain. The response to policy will be in the right direction, but whether the resulting acceleration of growth will be large or small, permanent or temporary, is beyond knowing.

Two options for growth-oriented policy appear in this picture. One is to aim for temporary increases in the growth rate, to accept that lifting the potential trend is ambitious and important. Then there are several policy directions, all leading in the right direction. Increases in investment will do the trick, and the menu includes increases in plant-and-equipment investment; in human-capital investment through education and training; in public investment in the infrastructure of transportation, communication, and information flow; and, of course, in research and development. The second option is to seek higher growth rates on a long-term basis. Then the theory says that only the research-and-development-and-entrepreneurship path is a candidate and one cannot know exactly—or even approximately—what will be required to achieve a measurable acceleration of steady-state growth.

It is worth mentioning an emerging problem here. Skilled people can migrate, and new technology can migrate even faster. So investment one country pays for can benefit primarily other countries, as in the case of brain drain, or can benefit other countries as well as the originating country, as in the case of technological imitation. The globalization of economic activity means that even a whole nation may be too small to "internalize the externality" and capture a large fraction of the return on its own investment. That is why, for example, disputes over "intellectual property rights" are now as prominent as disputes over conventional trade barriers. One can imagine three sorts of outcomes: either a satisfactory agreement will be reached on intellectual property rights, or ways will be found to internationalize the costs of all but the most narrowly proprietary research and development, or there will be serious attempts at secrecy and protection in the field of technology. Either of the first two outcomes would be preferable to the third; but there is no guarantee that the world will evolve in that direction.

I have been careful to talk about the growth theory of the 1950s and 1960s, the Old Growth Theory. More recently, since the mid-1980s, there has emerged a New Growth Theory, which comes to more than slightly different conclusions. The pioneers, as all economists know, were Paul Romer and Robert Lucas, but there is now a long list of contributors. The usual name for what is new about New Growth Theory is that the growth rate is "endogenous," which only means that it is determined within the theory rather than taken as a given. The reference is to the fact that in Old Growth Theory, the steady-state rate of growth is always essentially given by the rate of technological progress, which is not further explained. I think this label puts the emphasis in the wrong place. None of the Old Growth theorists ever believed the rate of technological progress to be independent of economic decisions and events. But, having nothing very specific to say about how it is determined, they simply took it as given. The sorts of things I said earlier about research and development decisions could have been said anytime, and no doubt were.

The real novelty in New Growth Theory is that each version—and there are several—rests on a strong assumption about production that gives investment decisions very great leverage on growth rates. Almost always the key assumption suspends the operation of diminishing returns on some factor of production that can be accumulated.

Sometimes this is done quite directly: in some models it is just assumed that there are increasing returns to physical capital. That means that increasing capital intensity, instead of using up the most productive and profitable opportunities for investment, actually creates more productive and profitable ones, although only a fraction of the return may be captured by the investor. Sometimes it is done indirectly: in some models it is assumed that there are increasing returns in the production of human capital (or knowledge), though not in its use. For instance, it may be supposed that a maintained increase in the *number* of hours per week devoted by the typical worker to education or training will permanently increase the *rate of growth* of the human capital thus generated. Sometimes the key assumption is quite subtle: in some models the source of increasing returns is not the quantity but the variety of productive inputs. It has been assumed, for example, that final output can be made to grow to infinity just by subdividing a fixed "amount" of intermediate inputs into an ever greater variety. In all the instances that I have seen, the operative assumption is quite powerful.

From powerful assumptions come powerful conclusions. And the results of New Growth Theory offer wide scope for growth-oriented policy. Two sorts of results emerge. In the first place it is shown that a sustained rise in the share of national income invested—in physical capital, say—can create a permanent increase in the economy's growth rate. This is just what the older theory denied. The difference is that in one story the grip of diminishing returns eventually prevails and in the other it does not. If the newer view is correct—and that remains to be discussed—the promotion of investment by tax or public-expenditure policy gives a direct and *permanent* push to the growth rate.

The second sort of result is very striking, too. It was a characteristic of Old Growth Theory that any sort of favorable or unfavorable event, as long as it was temporary, would have no effect on the ultimate long-run path of the economy. A temporary tax increase on the profits of capital would depress investment and growth as long as it stayed in place. But when it is removed, the economy gradually goes back to where it would have been if the tax change had never occurred. Similarly the sudden destruction of part of the stock of capital, by war or natural disaster, would, of course, make the economy poorer. But once again the economy would gradually return to the very same steady state it would have achieved if the flood had never occurred. This could be called Noah's Theorem. In the newer models that is no longer true. Even a temporary adverse shock to investment or a one-time loss of capital (or human capital) leaves major scars that never heal and may even get worse. If you imagine two identical island economies, one of which loses a quarter of its stock of capital to a storm that the other escapes, the fortunate island may have a permanent and widening advantage in income per head over its unlucky twin. One should always keep in mind that leverage for good is always accompanied by leverage for bad.

These models make policy both very powerful and very dangerous. Even if we remember firmly that words like "permanent" and "sustained" only mean "lasting a long time," the leverage of policy (and chance) on economic outcomes is great if the new ideas are true. It is even more significant that the range of policies with strong leverage is far broader than in the older sort of model. Depending on how the new-style model is formulated, it may be that investment in physical capital, or in human capital, or an easily achievable increase in the level of innovative activity can mean the difference between slower and faster growth in the long run. No one needs to be reminded that any noticeable difference in growth rates, sustained for a long time, cumulates to enormous differences in the level of income.

New Growth Theory has achieved extraordinary popularity among analytical economists. By itself that only means that it is intellectually exciting. New sorts of make-believe economies can be investigated; and they explain, or try to explain, parts of economic life that were formerly felt to be outside the scope of economic analysis. The power of the new results makes it all the more important to decide whether the powerful assumptions that lead to them are true. Before jumping to the policy conclusions, we must decide whether to accept them or to accept their foundations. It is, in fact, very hard to imagine how those assumptions can be tested directly.

As I have emphasized, the key assumptions all seem to require that some economic activity be exempt from diminishing returns. That is hard enough to test for a single industry or process, and even then might not settle the relevant question. Of course, some processes exhibit diminishing returns and some increasing returns. The problem is to know which is a better approximate representation for the economy as a whole. Another obstacle to empirical knowledge is that some activities whose nature we need to understand are intrinsically hard to define and to measure. This is especially true of activities meant to create human capital or usable technological knowledge, or variety in productive inputs or consumer goods. I do not know of any serious attempts to make such

tests or of any convincing evidence that would compel a normally skeptical person to accept—or confidently to reject—
those powerful assumptions and their implications. The tendency within economics has been to try something indirect
and, as we shall see, tricky. In the meanwhile, skepticism—
genuine open-minded skepticism—seems like the right atti-
tude.

A combination of circumstances has led to a new sort of
research aimed at uncovering the effective sources of growth.
One circumstance is precisely the emergence of the new sort
of theory that I have been discussing. If you suspect that the
growth rate responds sensitively to economic decisions, public and private, then it should be relatively easy to find traces
of these effects in the record of economic growth. Of course,
you need a record in which to search.

That is the second circumstance. A large body of data,
covering the experience of many countries over three or four
decades, is now available. The advantage of using data from
many countries is that the countries are not all alike. The
variety of policies and circumstances observed will be greater
than any single country will experience during its statistical history. The same is true of such nonpolicy differences
as changes in private behavior, international influences, and
chance events. So looking across countries is useful for the
same reason that the effects of differences in rainfall on crop
yields will be easier to discern if you can observe both arid
countries and rainy countries, instead of just wet years and
dry years in the same country.

The disadvantage of such bodies of data is that different
countries may not be comparable in some important respect.
The experience of very poor countries may not be relevant for
very rich countries, or the experience of agricultural coun-

tries may not be relevant for industrial countries. The experience of open economies may not be relevant to relatively self-contained economies. The experience of countries with strongly "corporatist" institutions may not be relevant to the experience of economies without such organization. The only answer one can give to that sort of question is to try and see whether consistent and meaningful results can be achieved. Every one of those possible differences can be converted into an explicit hypothesis and tested.

The other potential source of international incomparability is purely statistical. There are different methods of collecting data, different sorts of price indexes, sometimes even different definitions. If the effects we are trying to detect are fairly subtle, these statistical difficulties can easily obscure them. The good news is that two collections of international income and product statistics have been prepared for comparability. One is from the World Bank and the other from two American scholars, Robert Summers and Alan Heston, who provide data for as many as 138 countries for 30 years, even to the point of grading the quality of the data on a scale from A to D. The bad news is that the two bodies of data sometimes give inconsistent results. They are, however, our only source of extensive empirical knowledge. What do they show?

First, let me describe what is done in order to find out. Suppose you had a list of dietary habits, environmental characteristics, genetic factors, and perhaps other things, all of which might be expected to have an influence on the incidence of a disease like cancer. You want to find some way to assess their relative importance. One thing you might do is to collect information for a number of countries in the world on the incidence of cancer during some common period of time, as well as on each of the other characteristics — proportion of meat in the diet, use of tobacco, amount of direct sunshine, skin pigmentation, and so on. Well-known statistical techniques exist for calculating how closely the incidence of cancer by country is correlated with this group of national characteristics and for estimating how important each of them seems to be. Usually, of course, you do not get a complete "explanation" of the incidence of cancer in this way; there remains a lot of unexplained noise. But you may learn enough to matter.

The typical procedure is the same when the subject to be explained is national differences in rates of economic growth. One starts with growth rates of GDP or GDP per worker for many countries, averaged over a long enough period to eliminate the effects of short-term fluctuations. The other variables are taken from the list suggested by growth theory: rates of investment in plant and equipment and infrastructure, rates of investment in human capital—usually measured rather imperfectly by figures on school enrollment because that is what is available—and perhaps some figures on the industrial composition of GDP. Usually one includes the initial level of income, on the Old Growth Theory presumption that the poorer countries at the start have further to go than the others and will find it easier to make progress for that reason. (You may be surprised by that, but it almost always turns out to be so.)

It is interesting that many of the studies include descriptive characteristics that have little or no theoretical connection to the growth rate achieved but do measure the orderliness and coherence of economic policy: the average rate of inflation during the period, the size of a country's external debt, its budget deficit or surplus, even direct measures of political stability/instability. The range of countries in these studies usually goes all the way from very poor less-developed countries to very rich industrialized countries, and I suspect that these political characteristics play a role primarily for that reason. A high rate of inflation—generally negatively correlated with real growth—is as much an indicator of a government out of control as it is a reflection of the fact that rapid (and therefore variable) inflation interferes with the performance of the price mechanism in allocating resources and also creates risks that reduce the volume and efficiency of investment.

The first thing that must be said is that these statistical analyses do not settle conclusively the contest between Old Growth Theory and New. To my eye—which may not be neutral, because after all I am an Old Growth theorist—the international record suggests that there is no compelling need to invoke the new ideas. The data can be accounted for in a satisfactory way without them. (There is one very interesting amendment: something like half of the conventionally measured contribution of labor to the growth of output may be more specifically the contribution of human capital, the other half belonging to some sort of "standard" labor.) But the data are also reasonably compatible with New Growth Theory ideas, though perhaps not with the more explosive versions of them. It should not be surprising that the historical cross-country record is inconclusive. In the first place, some fraction of international differences in growth rates stems from idiosyncratic, unsystematic factors, pieces of good or bad luck, and the like, exactly as with international differences in the incidence of cancer. In the second place, the contrast between new and old in growth theory is not necessarily like the difference between black and white; there is a range of gray and, within the gray area, it is hard to discriminate.

Whichever way the theoretical question is eventually decided, the studies leave no doubt at all that investment—physical, human, and intellectual—matters for growth on a time scale of two or three decades. The issues are only matters of degree and duration. Even 30 years is not long enough to distinguish between temporary episodes of accelerated growth and increases in the growth rate itself. A society that wants to accelerate its growth must increase its stock of tangible and human capital faster and accelerate the entry of new technology into production. The payoff is not terribly dramatic, and it is uncertain—but it is there. I think it would be good for the accuracy and integrity of policy discussion if promises to raise the growth rate were replaced by promises to lift the trend. I have not been able to think of a catchy phrase for trend-lifting, but one would be welcome. Talk about growth rates should wait until it has a more reliable foundation. (Perhaps this is the place for me to say that all such promises should pay more respect to environmental and resource constraints than in the past. I do not want to be misunderstood. I think those constraints are of great importance, especially in a world characterized by enormous inequality between rich countries and poor. I simply have not emphasized environmental and resource constraints because I have nothing new or different to say about them.)

The international cross-section studies typically show that fiscal and monetary orderliness—low inflation, limited external debt, a reasonable budgetary stance—are also positively associated with economic growth. This sounds like a more significant conclusion than it is. It does not mean that the United States or France would automatically grow faster—or lift its trend—if its fiscal policy were a little tighter. What it seems to mean is that the growth performance of African and Latin American countries has been worse than the fundamentals would indicate. Those continents, more than others, have experienced inflation, indebtedness, and fiscal extravagance.

Modesty is a virtue in reading this evidence, not only because its scope is limited but because the statistical results themselves are fragile. This means that quite small changes in the model—so small that no one could treat them as a matter of principle—often lead to substantial changes in the story told by statistical analysis. It is not possible to be confident about what really lies behind the observed correlations.

For the developed economies, a reasonable interpretation is that the favorable effects of sound macroeconomic policy work mainly *through* investment. That is to say, inflation is bad for growth because inflation is bad for investment, and macroeconomic stability is good for growth because macroeconomic stability is good for investment. That is what vaguer notions like "confidence" come down to. Conscience requires me to repeat that all such inferences from international comparisons are shaky. What does stand out is the importance of physical, human, and technological investment, and the Old Growth Theory conclusion that, when account is taken of investment and technology, there remains some tendency within the group of industrial nations for the slightly poorer ones to catch up with the slightly richer ones.

Those conclusions are an adequate foundation for growth-oriented policy as long as one does not ask for too much. I mean two separate things under the heading of "asking too much." The first is to demand or to promise too much precision. Over the years economists have learned how to think about economic growth and have even been able to achieve some serious quantitative results. But the links between policy and action and between action and growth are uncertain and will probably remain uncertain, not because economists are stupid, but because life is like that. A mature democracy should learn that it can pursue growth through investment and technological development. But it cannot be sure exactly when the benefits will arrive and exactly how large they will be. Excessive demands from voters and rash promises by candidates are not a good basis for a commitment to a high-growth policy.

The other way of asking or promising too much is to focus too exclusively on tilting the potential trend instead of lifting it. New Growth Theory may turn out to be right in its main contentions. In that case it may point the way to powerful policy initiatives. But we are still a long way from any confidence that it is the case. For the present, a mature democracy should learn that the forces governing the slope of the potential trend—the sustainable rate of growth—are complex, mostly technological, and even a little mysterious. What we do know how to do is to lift the potential trend by a few percent. Even if the slope remains as before, that is a fine achievement. Its absolute significance, measured in constant dollars, gets bigger as time goes on. According to Summers and Heston, real GDP per worker in Mexico is 40 percent of that in the United States. Closing that gap, or even half of that gap, would be a historic change for the Mexican people and a worthy goal for 30 years or even longer. It is an interesting question whether realistic policy goals can become viable political platforms, either in Mexico or here. I wish I knew the answer, but why would you ask a theorist?

«»

BIBLIOGRAPHICAL NOTE

The place to begin, obviously, is with Arrow's paper, "The Economic Implications of Learning by Doing," *Review of Economic Studies* 28 (1962): 155–73. Further theoretical development is to be found in two papers by David Levhari: "Further Implications of Learning by Doing," *Review of Economic Studies* 33 (1967): 31–38, and "Extensions of Arrow's Learning by Doing," in the same issue of *Review of Economic Studies*, pp. 117–31. There is also some additional theory in Eytan Sheshinski's "Tests of the Learning-by-Doing Hypothesis," *Review of Economics and Statistics* 49 (1967): 568–78, although theory is not its main concern.

Empirical learning curves go back to the 1930s in the industrial engineering literature. The earliest reference I remember in economics is Werner Hirsch, "Manufacturing Progress Functions," *Review of Economics and Statistics* 34 (1952): 143–55. Another important empirical paper is Armen Alchian, "Reliability of Progress Curves in Airframe Production," *Econometrica* 31 (1963): 679–93, which reflects the work at RAND that inspired Arrow. An excellent recent survey of applications is Linda Argote and Dennis Epple, "Learning Curves in Manufacturing," *Science* 247 (1990): 920–24, which contains an extensive bibliography.

For uses of the idea in other branches of economics, namely labor economics and industrial organization, see Sherwin Rosen, "Learning by Experience as Joint Production," *Quarterly Journal of Economics* 86 (1972): 366–82, and Drew Fudenberg and Jean Tirole, "Learning by Doing and Market Performance," *Bell Journal* 14 (1983): 522–30. Finally, to come back to the original growth-theoretic construct, see Alwyn Young, "Learning by Doing and the Dynamic Effects of International Trade," *Quarterly Journal of Economics* 106 (1991): 369–406, and, most closely related to these lectures, Young's "Invention and Bounded Learning by Doing," *Journal of Political Economy* 101 (1993): 443–72.

Some additional sources are also cited in these chapters: Philippe Aghion and Peter Howitt, "A Model of Growth Through Creative Destruction," *Econometrica* 60 (1992): 323–51; Robert Solow, James Tobin, Christian von Weizäcker, and Menachem Yaari, "Neoclassical Growth with Fixed Factor Proportions," *Review of Economic Studies* 33 (1965): 79–115; Robert Summers and Alan Heston, "The Penn World Table (Mark 5): An Expanded Set of International Comparisons, 1950–1988," *Quarterly Journal of Economics* 106 (1991) 327–68.

Library of Congress Calaloging-in-Publication Data

Solow, Robert M.
  Learning from "learning by doing" : lessons for economic growth /
  Robert M. Solow.
     p.   cm. — (The Kenneth J. Arrow lectures)
  Includes bibliographical references (p.).
  ISBN 0-8047-2840-2 (cloth : alk paper). —
  ISBN 0-8047-2841-0 (pbk. : alk. paper)
  1. Economic development.   I. Title   II. Series.
  HD75.S6452   1997
  338.9 — dc20   96-31847
                                                               CIP

⊗   This book is printed on acid-free, recycled paper.

Original printing 1997
Last figure below indicates year of this printing

06   05   04   03   02   01   00   99   98   97